To Ron & Ja

TO BE HOOSIERS

HISTORIC STORIES OF CHARACTER & FORTITUDE

RAY E. BOOMHOWER

Merry Christmas 2020

Jayne & Dave

THE
History
PRESS

Published by The History Press
Charleston, SC
www.historypress.com

Front cover, clockwise from top left: Mercury astronaut Gus Grissom. *National Aeronautics and Space Administration*; poster advertising Indianapolis Motor Speedway. *Library of Congress*; President Benjamin Harrison. *Library of Congress*; Amelia Earhart with Purdue University students. *Purdue University Libraries, Kansas Archives and Special Collections*.

First published 2020

Manufactured in the United States

ISBN 9781467145404

Library of Congress Control Number: 2019951859

"Hoosier: He is a puzzling combination of shy provincial, unfettered democrat, and Fourth of July orator. He is a student by choice, a poet by sneaking inclination, and a storyteller by reason of his nativity."
—George Ade

To the finest Hoosier I know, and the person who has been the inspiration for all I have written: my wife, Megan L. McKee. She is my everything.

CONTENTS

WHAT IS A HOOSIER?

O n January 1, 1833, just seventeen years after Indiana became the nineteenth state in the Union, the *Indianapolis Journal*, as a New Year's greeting to its readers, printed in its "Carrier's Address" a poem by John Finley of Richmond, Indiana. Finley's poem, "The Hoosier's Nest," which praised the state and proclaimed that countless "men of every hue and fashion" were flocking to the "Hoosier nation," received instant acclaim and was reprinted in numerous newspapers throughout the country and even internationally.

Since that first appearance in the *Journal*, the term "Hoosier" has become one of America's most recognizable state nicknames—along with "Buckeyes" for those from Ohio, "Badgers" from Wisconsin, "Wolverines" from Michigan and "Tarheels" for North Carolina.

Throughout its history, Indiana has been seen by many, noted Indiana historian and journalist John Bartlow Martin, as "a bucolic place inhabited by pleasant, simple, neighborly folk." It was a state where a radical thinker like Eugene Debs—Hoosier union organizer, writer, lecturer and five-time presidential hopeful for the Socialist Party—could maintain close friendships with some of the richest men in his hometown of Terre Haute, as well as with a man considered as the prototypical Hoosier, poet James Whitcomb Riley.

This "Indiana idea," as Martin called it, contained "good deal of myth" and also masked from view the less desirable aspects of the Hoosier character, including a time in the 1920s when the Ku Klux Klan under D.C.

In his dialect poem "Regardin' Terre Hut," James Whitcomb Riley praised his friend Eugene Debs, writing, "And there's Gene Debs—a man 'at stands / And just holds out in his two hands / As warm a heart as ever beat / Betwixt here and the Jedgement seat." *Library of Congress.*

Stephenson controlled state government. Although the "Indiana idea" has undergone a metamorphosis, as rural and agriculture have been supplanted by urban and industrial, those ideas still have a powerful hold on the way in which Hoosiers view their past. "Like any myth," Martin noted, "it has some truth in it."

One question about the state always seems to linger in the back of the minds of visitors: "What *is* a Hoosier?" Since Finley's poem popularized the term, speculation about the origin of Hoosier has run rampant. The late Indiana historian Jacob Piatt Dunn Jr. conducted lengthy research into the history of the word. Dunn found out that Hoosier was used frequently in the South in the nineteenth century to refer to woodsmen or rough hill people. He traced the word back to *hoozer*, a term from the Cumberland dialect of England. Hoozer is from the Anglo-Saxon word *hoo*, meaning "high or hill." In the Cumberland dialect, the word *hoozer* meant anything unusually large, like a hill. Descendants of English immigrants brought the name with them when they settled in the hill country of southern Indiana.

Other theories abound as to the origin of Hoosier, providing the following entertaining anecdotes:

- When a visitor knocked on the door of a pioneer cabin in Indiana, the settler inside would respond, "Who's yere?" This greeting marked Indiana as the "Who's yere" or Hoosier state.
- Indiana laborers along the Ohio River were so successful in trouncing or "hushing" their opponents in fights that they became known as "hushers" and, eventually, Hoosiers.
- There once existed a contractor named Hoosier working on the Louisville and Portland Canal who hired most of his laborers from Indiana. Thereafter they were known as "Hoosier's men."
- Riley claimed that the state's early settlers were such enthusiastic and vicious fighters that during scuffles they would do anything to win, including biting off noses and ears. A settler coming into a tavern the morning after a fight would encounter missing appendages on the ground and ask, "Whose ear?"
- Indiana author and diplomat Meredith Nicholson had perhaps the best response to the query "What is a Hoosier?" He noted that the "origin of the term 'Hoosier' is not known with certainty. But certain it is that…Hoosiers bear their nickname proudly."

The puzzle about the meaning of Hoosier has stirred not only scholarly debate but controversy as well. In 1987, the office of then U.S. Senator Dan Quayle engaged in a battle with *Webster's Third International Dictionary* about its definition of the word. In its alternative meanings for Hoosier, the dictionary defined the noun form as "an awkward, unhandy or unskilled person, especially an ignorant rustic." The verb form meant, the dictionary added, "to loaf on or botch a job."

New York senator Alfonse D'Amato even used the dictionary's uncomplimentary definition to predict defeat for Indiana University in its battle for the National Collegiate Athletic Association basketball championship against Syracuse University that year. (Thanks to guard Keith Smart's timely last-second shot, IU prevailed, 74–73.)

Quayle's press secretary, Peter M. Lincoln, struck back at Merriam-Webster Inc. by threatening to remove the dictionary from the senator's office unless the company changed its definition for Hoosier. Lincoln also invented a new word, *webster*, whose form meant "to mis-define a word

President Ronald Reagan (*left*) talks to U.S. Senator Dan Quayle of Indiana at his desk in the Oval Office of the White House, Washington, D.C., 1986. *Photographs in the Carol M. Highsmith Archive, Library of Congress, Prints and Photographs Division.*

stubbornly and outrageously. The people of Merriam-Webster are guilty of 'webstering.'"

The search for the meaning of the word Hoosier continues. In 1995, William D. Piersen, Fisk University professor of history, in an article for the *Indiana Magazine of History*, theorized that the term Hoosier came from an itinerant African American minister named Harry Hoosier, a former slave called by one Methodist clergyman "one of the best Preachers in the world." Accepting his theory, Piersen wrote, would "offer Indiana a plausible and worthy first Hoosier—'Black Harry' Hoosier—the greatest preacher of his day, a man who rejected slavery and stood up for morality and the common man."

The final answer to "What is a Hoosier?" may never be known, but there are, at least, ways to understand the character of those from the state by examining, as I do in this collection, events and people from the past. These include a stand by African American pilots for their equal rights, a speech by a presidential candidate that helped keep peace on a tragic night, the triumph and near tragedy involving Indiana's first astronaut and the sacrifice made to ensure an American victory at a turning point in the Pacific during World War II. As Kurt Vonnegut once said, "I don't know what it is about Hoosiers, but wherever you go there is always a Hoosier doing something very important there."

BALLOONS OVER THE SPEEDWAY

On a balmy June weekend in 1909, thousands of Indianapolis residents piled into their cars for what would be in the years to come a familiar trip to a track on the city's west side: the Indianapolis Motor Speedway. The crowd had gathered, however, not to witness men racing automobiles around the two-and-a-half-mile oval, but rather to marvel at the daredevil antics of aeronauts willing to risk their lives in a national hot air balloon race.

The promotional wizard behind the event was no stranger to attracting attention to himself. Born in Greensburg, Indiana, Carl Fisher had quit school at a young age in order to support his family. Over the years, he had worked at several professions, including clerking in a bookstore and hawking newspapers, candy and other products on trains leaving Indianapolis. In 1891, he and his two brothers opened a bicycle shop in Indianapolis, where they repaired flat tires for just twenty-five cents. When the automotive craze swept the country, Fisher jumped on the bandwagon, converting his bicycle shop into an automobile repair/sales facility and barnstorming through the Midwest with his friends putting on automotive races.

To promote his new product, Fisher staged a series of crazy stunts sure to earn him plenty of attention in Indianapolis newspapers. On one occasion, while his brothers waited on the street below, he shoved a seven-passenger car off a building's roof. When the car safely reached the street, one of Fisher's brothers climbed into the car, started it up and drove away with the crowd's cheers ringing in his ears.

Carl G. Fisher had a simple method for doing business: "I have a great many men working for me who I consider have more brain power than I have, and I always try to get this type of men to aid me. It pays well in any sort of business to know all your employees, from the truck drivers up—and to stick by them in any sort of trouble." *Bretzman Collection, Indiana Historical Society.*

On a 1905 overseas trip to compete in the Gordon Bennett Cup Series in France, Fisher was stunned by the European cars' superiority over the American models. To help improve the automotive industry back home, he conceived of a proving ground where cars could be tested and raced. In 1909, Fisher, Arthur Newby, Frank Wheeler and James Allison put together $25,000 in capital to form the Indianapolis Motor Speedway Company and transformed the Pressley Farm into one of the country's premier auto racing tracks.

Before cars took to the track, however, Fisher had the idea of christening the facility by sponsoring a national championship balloon race on June 5, 1909. This was not the first time Fisher had used balloons for publicizing one of his ventures. Just the year before, with his friend George Bumbaugh of Springfield, Illinois, Fisher had inflated a large balloon and attached to it a Stoddard-Dayton automobile. Indianapolis residents were astonished to look up on the late afternoon of October 30, 1908, to see an automobile sailing through the sky, with Fisher waving at them from the driver's seat.

Sanctioned by the Aero Club of America, the Indianapolis balloon competition featured nine balloons entered in two categories. Three were featured in the handicap race for balloons with capacities of forty thousand cubic feet: the *Ohio*, the *Indianapolis* (piloted by Indianapolis physician Goethe Link and his friend J.R. "Russy" Irwin) and the *Chicago*. Entered in the national contest for balloons with capacities of eighty thousand cubic feet were the *New York*, *Indiana* (manned by Fisher and Bumbaugh), *Saint Louis III*, *Cleveland*, *Hoosier* and *University City*. In order to fill the craft to the proper size, Fisher had a special gas main run from the main Indianapolis gas plant near Northwestern Avenue and Fall Creek to the Speedway location.

On Saturday afternoon, June 5, the balloons rose into the air as more than forty thousand fans cheered. The crush of spectators was so great that Indiana governor Thomas Marshall could not reach the location in time to serve as the contest's official starter. As Fisher's craft floated over the grandstand, where spectators had paid one dollar each for their seats, he threw a number of American beauty roses to the crowd that had been sent to him by his mother. Asked for his opinion about the event as the last balloon had left the ground for parts unknown, Charles J. Glidden, noted industrialist and one of the chief founders of the Aero Club, called it "without doubt the most beautiful and the best conducted that human eyes have ever witnessed."

Those entered in the race were seeking to remain in the air the longest and to travel the farthest distance. As day turned to night, Link remembered

Above: A crowd watches participants prepare their craft for the start of the National Balloon Race at the Indianapolis Motor Speedway, June 5, 1909. *Bass Photo Company Collection, Indiana Historical Society.*

Opposite: Writing about the race for the *Indianapolis Star*, Fisher noted that at "the height of 4,000 feet the Speedway grounds presented an inspiring sight, as we could see thousands of men and women waving us a last good-by and wishing us good luck." *Bass Photo Company Collection, Indiana Historical Society.*

riding over a forest in southern Indiana, skimming over the treetops and dragging from the balloon a three-hundred-foot-long drag rope that slammed into a house and made a noise that could be heard for miles. "I wondered what those people thought it was," said Link. As the aeronauts left Indiana for the states of Kentucky and Tennessee, they began to come under fire from frightened farmers armed with shotguns and rifles. The gunfire caused Link and Irwin to ascend to a height of almost three miles. Gasping for breath due to the thin supply of oxygen and shivering from the cold even while wrapped in an overcoat and blanket, Irwin noted, "If I ever get out of this alive, I'll never do this again."

The two men survived their ordeal and finally landed at 11:15 a.m. on Sunday near Westmoreland, Tennessee. In winning the handicap race, for which they received an engraved silver cup, the duo had been in the air for about nineteen hours and had traveled 250 miles. Before landing, Link had to lighten the balloon's load by throwing out a full lunch basket. Some of the local residents volunteered to retrieve the lost lunch for the hungry aeronauts, but when the basket was returned to them, they discovered that ants had invaded their provisions. Link and Irwin returned to Indianapolis the next day after a breakfast of hardboiled eggs.

The national contest ended in controversy. Fisher and Bumbaugh in the *Indiana* had remained in the air for forty-eight hours and thirty minutes, finally landing near Tennessee City, Tennessee, about fifty miles from Nashville, on Monday evening. As had Link and Irwin, Fisher and Bumbaugh had become targets for trigger-happy people on the ground. "They began firing on us when we were in Brown County, Indiana, and

have kept up the target practice ever since—right up to six o'clock Monday evening, when we stepped out of the basket," Fisher said in a telephone interview with an *Indianapolis Star* reporter. The gunfire increased in volume as the balloon made its way to Tennessee. "No more ballooning in Tennessee for me," Fisher vowed.

The controversy occurred when Fisher and Bumbaugh had brought their balloon in for a landing on a pile of railroad crossties four feet off the ground in order to take on a supply of water. Fisher argued that because the balloon had never touched ground, and he and Bumbaugh had remained in the basket, they were within the rules of the contest. Other contestants, and Aero Club officials, disagreed with Fisher's reasoning. Nevertheless, the two were treated as heroes when they returned to Indianapolis on an interurban car from Louisville. A crowd of more than two hundred people greeted the aeronauts, who were treated to a parade complete with a band and fireworks before a banquet in their honor at the Denison Hotel. The crowd serenaded the men with the following chant: "Fisher and Bumbaugh, they're the stuff, / Fisher and Bumbaugh, they're no bluff. / Sure they came down before they oughter, / But only to get a bucket of water."

INDIANA'S FAVORITE SON

BENJAMIN HARRISON

On a fall day in 1888, the sound of marching feet echoed through the streets of Indianapolis. Armed with red, white and blue parasols and led by drummers from eleven states, a crowd of about forty thousand commercial travelers marched up North Delaware Street to call on a local lawyer, who happened to be the Republican nominee for president. As the attorney and his wife appeared at the front door of their sixteen-room Italianate Victorian mansion, the travelers responded with "cheers upon cheers," one eyewitness, Mary Lord Dimmick, remembered later. The cheers lasted until the attorney spoke, she said, and "then…you could have heard a pin drop."

The crowds that flocked to Indianapolis in 1888 came to visit a man who, from an early age, seemed destined for political life. Benjamin Harrison was the son of John Scott Harrison, a two-term congressman from Ohio; grandson of William Henry Harrison, the first governor of the Indiana Territory and ninth president of the United States; and the great-grandson of Benjamin Harrison V, governor of Virginia and a signer of the Declaration of Independence. Benjamin Harrison captured the presidency that year, defeating incumbent Grover Cleveland.

The future twenty-third president was born on his grandfather's farm at North Bend, Ohio, on August 20, 1833. After receiving his early education at Farmers' College in Cincinnati, Harrison graduated from Miami University in Oxford, Ohio, in 1852. After graduation, the young man studied law for two years with a Cincinnati firm and married Caroline Lavinia Scott, an

Benjamin Harrison had a clear understanding of the stress serving as president entailed, once noting, "I have often thought the life of the President is like that of the policeman in the opera, not a happy one." *Library of Congress.*

Oxford Female Institute graduate and an accomplished artist and musician. In 1854, the twenty-one-year-old Harrison and his wife moved to the growing city of Indianapolis, and Harrison established his own law practice.

Given Hoosiers' love of politics, and the famous Harrison name, the young lawyer became drawn—somewhat reluctantly—into the political scene. In 1856, while busy working at his law office, Harrison was interrupted by some Republican friends who dragged him from his office to speak before a political gathering. Introduced to the crowd as the grandson of "Old Tippecanoe," Harrison firmly replied, "I want it understood that I am the grandson of nobody. I believe that every man should stand on his own merits."

The Harrison family's strong political background, however, did aid young Harrison as he undertook a political career, becoming Indianapolis city attorney in 1857 and being elected to the post of Indiana Supreme Court reporter three years later. The Civil War halted Harrison's political career. Asked by Indiana governor Oliver P. Morton to recruit men for the Seventieth Indiana Volunteer Infantry, Harrison served as a colonel with that outfit and offered sterling service to the Union cause in the Battles of Peach Tree Creek and Resaca, Georgia. During the war, Harrison received the nickname "Little Ben" from his troops (he stood five feet, six inches tall).

In a one-month period during the Union's fight to take Atlanta, Harrison, now in charge of a brigade of regiments that included the Seventieth, had participated in more battles than his grandfather William Henry Harrison had fought during his lifetime. At New Hope Church, Georgia, Harrison had his troops fix bayonets to attack the enemy position. "Men, the enemy's works are just ahead of us, but we will go right over them. Forward! Double-quick! March!" he ordered.

After a bloody action at Golgotha Church near Kennesaw Mountain on June 15—fighting in which two or three of his men had their heads torn off down to their shoulders—Harrison pitched in to help with the wounded, as the brigade's surgeons had scattered in the fighting. "Poor fellows!" Harrison said of the casualties who had taken shelter in a frame house. "I was but an awkward surgeon of course, but I hope I gave them some relief," he wrote Caroline. The colonel treated some "ghastly wounds," including pulling from a soldier's arm a "splinter five or six inches long and as thick as my three fingers." He also ordered tents to be torn up so the strips of cloth could be used to bandage the wounded.

Mustered out of the Grand Army of the Republic with a brevet brigadier general's commission, Harrison returned to Indianapolis to fill out his term as Indiana Supreme Court reporter before returning to his private law practice. Paradoxically for Harrison, as his biographer, Harry J. Sievers, noted, the financial panic that gripped the country in the early 1870s aided his firm, as "defaults, mortgage foreclosures, and bankruptcy cases flooded the office."

Financially secure, Harrison turned his attention to building a new home for his family, which included at that time two teenage children, Russell and Mary. In 1867, Harrison had purchased at auction a double lot on North Delaware Street, and it was here that the family's new red brick home was built during the fall and winter of 1874 and 1875 at a cost of about $20,000. Along with a library for Harrison's substantial book collection, the home possessed a ballroom and became a popular location for society events, including Thursday afternoon teas hosted by Caroline Scott Harrison, first president-general of the Daughters of the American Revolution.

In 1876, Harrison returned to the political arena, running as the GOP candidate for Indiana governor. He lost to Democrat James "Blue Jeans" Williams; his electoral failure, however, did not hurt his strong standing with Hoosier Republicans. In 1881, the Indiana legislature, controlled by the GOP, elected Harrison to serve a six-year term in the United States Senate. Harrison arrived on the national scene at an opportune time, as Indiana was

GENERAL BENJAMIN HARRISON.

Lithograph depicting Harrison, a Union army general, urging his men forward at the Battle of Resaca in the Civil War. *Library of Congress.*

playing a prominent role on the national political scene following the Civil War. To attract Hoosier voters, political parties often selected "favorite sons" from Indiana to bolster the parties' chances in November.

In 1888, the Republican Party nominated Harrison as its presidential candidate. Like most presidential contenders of that time, Harrison refused to barnstorm around the country for votes, preferring instead to remain at home. "I have a great risk of meeting a fool at home," he told journalist Whitelaw Reid, "but the candidate who travels cannot escape him."

While Cleveland remained in the White House, content with his duties as president and believing in the dictum "the office sought the man," Harrison embarked on a busy speaking schedule that saw him give more than eighty extemporaneous talks to more than 300,000 visitors to Indianapolis from July 7 to October 25. Usually, there were anywhere from one to three delegations per day, but at one point Harrison met seven on one day. To meet the demand posed by those who clamored to see the candidate at his Indianapolis home, a "committee of arrangements" was formed to manage the deluge of letters sent to Harrison and to schedule and control visitors.

The crowds, however, soon overwhelmed the space at the Delaware Street house and instead were moved about a mile away to University Park, the former drilling ground for Union soldiers. Marching bands were on hand at Union Station to welcome delegations as they arrived and accompanied them as they walked to the park. All the remarks made by outside groups were closely scrutinized to ensure that no controversial statements were uttered, and Harrison listened to them and often adjusted his speech to reflect what had been covered. Delegations included such groups as commercial travelers, Union war veterans, railroad workers, African American supporters, young girls who had formed a Harrison Club and old followers of William Henry Harrison's 1840 presidential campaign.

Although at the beginning of the campaign Harrison had called for the two parties to "encamp upon the high plains of principle and not in the low swamps of personal defamation or detraction," his hopes were dashed by the 1888 election's two great controversies—one that damaged Cleveland's chances and one that hurt Harrison. The first broadside came in October with what became known as the Murchison Letter. A California Republican had sent a letter, signed as Charles F. Murchison, to Sir Lionel Sackville-West, the British minister (ambassador) to the United States, asking his advice on how to vote. Not suspecting a trap, Sackville-West answered the letter with friendly words and support for the Cleveland administration as the best choice for British interests despite recent tensions over a dispute

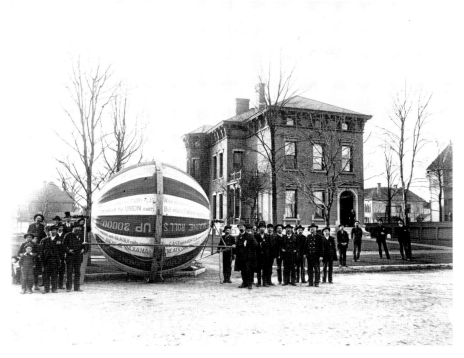

D.E. Brocket of Cumberland, Maryland, designed and built a steel-rigged and canvas-covered campaign ball to promote Harrison's 1888 campaign. Brocket took the ball on a five-thousand-mile trip, ending up at the candidate's Indianapolis home. *Indiana Historical Society, P0482.*

regarding fishing rights in Canada. Republican officials released Sackville-West's letter to the press. The seemingly friendly relations between the hated British and the Cleveland administration infuriated Irish American voters in New York, and Cleveland had to call for Sackville-West to be dismissed.

Shortly after the Murchison Letter had caused such a furor, the Democrats struck political gold with another letter, this one involving William W. Dudley, the Republican National Committee treasurer, and featuring the class of voter known as a "floater," a person with no fixed party allegiance who sold his ballot to the highest bidder, be it Republican or Democrat. Party workers could buy these votes for as little as two dollars or as high as twenty dollars in close elections, and since political parties, not the state, printed and furnished ballots to voters, this ensured that once a "floater" was bought, he stayed bought. "This infamous practice," complained the *Shelbyville Republican*, "kept up year after year by both parties, has brought about a state of affairs that cannot be contemplated without a shudder." The newspaper went on to lament that one-third of the state's voting population "can be directly influenced by the use of money on the day of election."

In a letter sent to an Indiana Republican county chairman, Dudley warned that "only boodle and fraudulent votes and false counting of returns can beat us in the State [Indiana]." To counter this threat, he advised Republican workers to find out which Democrats at the polls were responsible for bribing voters and steer committed Democratic supporters to them, thereby exhausting the opposition's cash stockpile. The most damaging part of the letter, however, appeared in a sentence where Dudley advised, "Divide the voters into blocks of five, and put a trusted man, with necessary funds, in charge of these five, and make them responsible that none get away."

The political dynamite in Dudley's letter found its way to the opposition thanks to a Democratic mail clerk on the Ohio and Mississippi Railroad who was suspicious about the large amount of mail being passed from Republican headquarters to Indiana Republicans. He opened one of the letters, recognized its value to his party and passed the damaging contents to the Indiana Democratic State Central Committee. The *Sentinel* printed the letter on October 31, 1888, under a banner headline reading, "The Plot to Buy Indiana." Although an indignant Dudley and other top Republican officials declared that the letter was a forgery and denounced the person responsible for interfering with the mail, its contents received nationwide attention, with newspapers supporting the Democratic cause, including the *Sentinel*, happy to lambaste Harrison for his ties to such chicanery, while Republican papers defended their candidate's character. Louis T. Michener, a Republican political veteran, pointed out that the instructions Dudley outlined were standard practice by both parties in Indiana and found nothing in the letter "unusual, illegal or immoral."

What effect both scandals had on the campaign's outcome is still debated by historians, with Charles Calhoun, in his book on the 1888 election, arguing that underhanded practices by both parties in New York and Indiana "may well have canceled each other out." Whatever the impact nationally, in Indiana the Dudley letter failed to dampen the enthusiasm of Hoosier Republicans for their favorite son. The day before the election, Harrison, on his way to his downtown law office, was greeted with applause and cheering. On Election Day, Tuesday, November 6, Harrison walked from his home, accompanied by his son, Russell, to Coburn's Livery Stable at Seventh Street between Delaware and Alabama Streets, the polling place for the Third Precinct of the Second Ward. To a cry from a supporter of

"There comes the next President," Harrison cast the ballot he had carried with him from his home.

After voting, Harrison returned home to learn his fate as a candidate, with regular reports coming to him in his library through a special telegraph wire connecting him with Republican headquarters in New York. After the polls closed, downtown streets in Indianapolis were clogged with people eager to hear the results, with many gathering near newspaper offices to receive reports. "As the morning drew nearer," noted an article in the *Indianapolis Journal*, "the wild crowd, growing hilarious with excitement, would receive a return with cheers, and the next moment follow it up with a refrain of 'Bye, Grover, bye; O, good-bye, old Grover, good-bye.' Another return, and 'What's the matter with Harrison? He's all right.'"

Several people gathered around a large, oval writing table in Harrison's library to read over the returns. When vote totals arrived over the wire from New York, they were read aloud, sometimes by Harrison and sometimes by his law partners, while Russell sorted bulletins by state. The *Journal* described the scene as "a quiet gathering of a few neighbors," adding that Harrison seemed "cool and self-possessed," sometimes retreating to the parlor to talk with his wife, Caroline, and her guests. According to one account, when returns from the state of New York seemed discouraging, Harrison took the news well, telling his friends to cheer up. "This is no life and death affair. I am very happy here in Indianapolis and will continue to be if I'm not elected. Home is a pretty good place."

Harrison seemed much more concerned about whether he won Indiana, closely perusing returns from each of the state's ninety-two counties. When his son-in-law, at about 11:00 p.m., announced that it looked as if Indiana had been won, Harrison responded, "That's enough for me tonight then. My own State is for me. I'm going to bed." At the White House, Cleveland also monitored the election results. At midnight in Washington, D.C., Secretary of the Navy William Collins Whitney walked out of the telegraph room and down a corridor to announce, "Well, it's all up." Asked the next morning how he could go to sleep still not knowing whether he had won the presidency, Harrison noted that his staying up would not have changed the results if he had lost, and if he won he knew he "had a hard day ahead of me. So I thought a night's rest was best in any event."

The Hoosier candidate won the presidency, securing the Electoral College with 233 votes to 168 for Cleveland. Harrison had been able to grab the crucial states of New York and Indiana, winning both by the barest of margins (by 2,376 votes in the Hoosier State and 14,373 votes

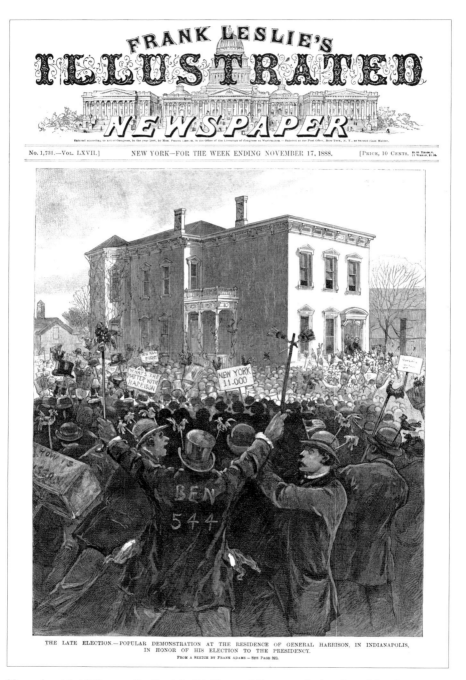

November 17, 1888 cover for *Frank Leslie's Illustrated Newspaper* depicts the celebration at Harrison's home following his election as the twenty-third president of the United States. *Indiana Historical Society, P0482.*

in New York; in both states, turnout exceeded 90 percent); both of these were states that Cleveland had captured in the 1884 election. In the popular vote, Cleveland bested Harrison, with 5,534,488 votes to 5,443,892 for his opponent, becoming the third of five presidential candidates to win the popular vote but lose in the Electoral College (the other losing candidates were Andrew Jackson in 1824, Samuel Tilden in 1876, Al Gore in 2000 and Hillary Clinton in 2016).

Harrison had firm beliefs in the policies of the Republican Party possessing the best means to improve life for the nation's citizens and worked to promote them as an activist, hands-on chief executive for both domestic matters and foreign affairs. "I do not know how our institutions could endure," he said, "unless we so conduct our public affairs and society that every man who is sober and industrious shall be able to make a good, comfortable living and lay something aside for old age and evil days; to have hope in their heart and better prospects for his children.…Whatever promotes that I want to favor." Harrison took on additional responsibilities in foreign affairs due to the poor health of Secretary of State James G. Blaine. As an Indianapolis newspaper noted, the president possessed "higher views of the functions of administration than the beaten path of routine and precedent." Harrison's administration had some impressive achievements, including passage of the Sherman Antitrust Act to limit business monopolies, the admission of six western states into the Union in 1889 and 1890, the establishment of 13 million acres for forest reserves and national parks, modernizing the American navy and negotiating several trade agreements with other countries.

During his administration, Harrison also sought to improve voting rights for African Americans—an act one historian called "the most courageous stand by any president of his era in favor of black Americans." In his message to Congress in December 1889, Harrison asked, "When and under what conditions is the black man to have a free ballot? When is he in fact to have those full civil rights which had so long been his in law? When is that equality of influence which our form of government was intended to secure to the electors to be restored?" Harrison backed up these strong words with action, appointing legendary African American social reformer and ex-slave Frederick Douglass as U.S. minister (today ambassador) to Haiti, as well as William D. McCoy, an Indianapolis black leader, as U.S. minister to Liberia. Unfortunately, legislation authorizing federal oversight of Congressional contests to ensure that African American voters would receive equal treatment failed in the Senate, but Harrison's effort in that regard "should endear him to the colored people as long as he lives," said Douglass.

As first lady, Caroline Scott Harrison also added luster to her husband's administration, fighting to improve a White House that had fallen into disrepair and advocating on behalf of the fine arts. In addition, she worked to secure admission for women into the Johns Hopkins Medical School and served as the first president-general of a fledgling organization—the Daughters of the American Revolution, which had been formed after the Sons of the American Revolution had declined to admit women applicants. Since its formation in 1890, the DAR has worked to secure and preserve "the historical spots of America and the erection thereon of suitable monuments to perpetuate the memories of the heroic deeds of the men and women who aided the revolution and created constitutional government in America."

No less an authority than Henry Adams, the distinguished historian and diplomat, considered Harrison to be "an excellent President, a man of ability and force; perhaps the best President the Republican Party had put forward since [Abraham] Lincoln's death." For all of his achievements, however, Harrison faced an uphill fight when he sought another four years in office, running for a second term once again with Cleveland as his opponent. Harrison had even faced some opposition from within his own party, including a possible run by his former secretary of state, James G. Blaine.

Although Republican officials wanted the president to undertake an aggressive campaign, he could not, as his wife was battling an illness—tuberculosis—that eventually led to her death on October 25, 1892. "Politics and business have been crowding me day and night," Harrison wrote his daughter, "and with the anxiety about your mother, makes life just now a burden and ambition a delusion." Harrison had even considered refusing to run for a second term; responding to slurs against his leadership, he had decided to persevere, telling a political ally, "No Harrison has ever retreated in the presence of a foe without giving battle, and so I have determined to stand and fight."

The Republicans' legislative efforts had been blocked when the party lost in midterm elections in 1890. Labor unrest two years later in the steel industry and at silver mines in the West hurt the incumbent's campaign, as did a last-minute announcement from leading Hoosier Republican (and Harrison rival) Walter Q. Gresham that he had decided to support the Democratic presidential candidate. Harrison lost his rematch with Cleveland, losing both the popular vote and in the Electoral College, 277 to 145; the president even lost his home state, Indiana, as well as such pivotal states as New York, New Jersey and Connecticut. Cleveland also captured Illinois and Wisconsin, the

Right: An 1889 portrait of First Lady Caroline Harrison, who did much to improve the White House during her husband's four years in office. *Library of Congress.*

Below: Harrison (*center*) and his secretary of state, James G. Blaine (*left*), relax while on vacation in Bar Harbor, Maine. *Library of Congress.*

first post–Civil War Democrat to do so. Harrison seemed almost relieved about his defeat, noting that the result was more "surprising to the victor than to me. For me there is not sting in it. Indeed after the heavy blow the death of my wife dealt me I do not think I could have stood the strain a re-election would have brought."

Harrison received a hero's welcome upon his return to Indianapolis, where he reestablished a flourishing law practice. As an ex-president, Harrison kept busy by preparing lectures on constitutional law for Stanford University, helping to propel the young institution to national prominence; writing articles about voting that appeared in the *Ladies' Home Journal*, one of the country's leading magazines; serving as a trustee for Purdue University; and representing the Republic of Venezuela in a border dispute with Great Britain. In that time, he refused all attempts to get him to run again for public office. "I do not see anything but labor and worry and distress in another campaign or another term in the White House," he said. At the age of sixty-two in 1896, he found personal happiness in a second marriage, with Mary Scott Dimmick, the widowed niece of his deceased wife, with whom he had a daughter, Elizabeth.

In early 1901, Harrison fell sick with influenza that later worsened into pneumonia. He died on March 13 in his Indianapolis home at the age of sixty-seven. According to his obituary in the *New York Times*, the former president's "death was quiet and painless, there being a gradual sinking until the end came, which was marked by a single gasp for breath as life departed from the body of the great statesman." At Harrison's funeral at Indianapolis's First Presbyterian Church, and before his eventual burial at Crown Hill Cemetery in a grave next to his first wife, Caroline, he was eulogized by another Indiana legend, the Hoosier poet himself, James Whitcomb Riley. One particular characteristic Harrison possessed impressed Riley: "[H]is fearless independence and stand for what he believed to be right and just….A fearless man inwardly commands respect, and above everything else Harrison was fearless and just."

CELEBRATING STATEHOOD

INDIANA AT 100

The fall of 1914 was a bloody one in Europe. The British and Germans were winding down the First Battle of Ypres and would soon dig in to begin the long and futile period of trench warfare. On the other side of the Atlantic Ocean, however, it was an election year. On November 3, Hoosiers trooped to the polls and "for a time the war dropped into the background as all Indiana played the election game," wrote Cedric C. Cummins in his book on public opinion during World War I.

In addition to the usual candidates on the ballot, voters had the chance to register their opinions on two special issues: a convention to alter the state's constitution and whether to celebrate the state's centennial in 1916 by appropriating $2 million for the construction of a memorial building to house the state library and other historical agencies. Both measures suffered defeat at the polls.

Democratic governor Samuel M. Ralston, who became a leading force behind the state's eventual centennial observance, believed that the memorial plan was rejected not because Hoosiers were against celebrating the event, but because they objected to the amount of money sought for the building.

Ralston was proven right; in just two years, backed by the efforts of the Indiana Historical Commission and thousands of volunteers, Indiana residents would see the creation of state parks, the beginnings of an improved statewide road system, the creation of permanent memorials in numerous communities and an overall awakening of interest in the nineteenth state's history.

Indiana's centennial governor, Samuel M. Ralston, does paperwork in his office at the statehouse in Indianapolis, March 1915. *Bass Photo Company Collection, Indiana Historical Society.*

At Governor Ralston's request, the 1915 Indiana General Assembly agreed to appropriate $25,000 and create a nine-member Indiana Historical Commission to promote the centennial celebration. The legislature's financial support of the commission marked the first notable state commitment of funds to history in Indiana. Of the $25,000, $20,000 was earmarked for the promotion of centennial activities, while the remaining amount went to collecting, editing and publishing Indiana's past.

The IHC first met on April 23 and 24, 1915, in Governor Ralston's statehouse office. An illustrious group joined Ralston on the commission, including James Woodburn of Indiana University, Reverend John Cavanaugh of the University of Notre Dame and Charity Dye, an Indianapolis schoolteacher. The commission employed professor Walter C. Woodward of Earlham College to direct the centennial celebration.

The commission set out to educate the state's citizens about the centennial. Special bulletins were sent to county school superintendents asking for their cooperation; direct appeals were made to teachers in the summer and fall of 1915; a weekly IHC newsletter began publication; and commission members addressed various clubs, civic organizations, churches and historical societies (Dye alone gave 152 talks).

The IHC also turned to film to get its message across to the public. Realizing that it had neither the necessary funds nor the skills needed to undertake such an enterprise, the commission called on the public for help. Citizens soon responded by forming the Inter-State Historical Pictures Corporation, which contracted with the Selig Polyscope Company of Chicago to produce a movie titled *Indiana*. The seven-reel picture featured famed poet James Whitcomb Riley telling the story of the state's development to a group of children.

To encourage former Indiana residents to return to the state for the centennial, the commission used the services of noted humorist and author George Ade. Honored, or "burdened," as Ade joked in speeches touting the centennial, with the chairmanship of the committee to "sound the call and bring all the wandering Hoosiers back into the fold," he set about recruiting contributions from a veritable who's who of Hoosiers for a book.

Titled *An Invitation to You and Your Folks from Jim and Some More of the Home Folks*, the book, published by Bobbs-Merrill Company of Indianapolis, contained messages from Governor Ralston, Vice President Thomas Marshall, Meredith Nicholson and Booth Tarkington. Gene Stratton-Porter contributed the poem "A Limberlost Invitation" and Riley the poem "The Hoosier in Exile."

With its publicity campaign on its way to being a success, the commission had to turn its sights to how best to stage the actual celebration; keeping in mind the lack of funds, it was clear that such events would have to be financed locally. The IHC turned to staging historical pageants. These dramas appealed strongly to the commission because they could both focus attention on Indiana's history and bring communities together.

The commission hired William Chauncy Langdon, former first president of the American Pageant Association, as the state pageant master. Langdon's main duties were to write and direct three pageants: one at Indiana University, another at the old state capital of Corydon and a final one at Indianapolis. Historical studies were made, music was specially composed and costumes were designed "for the sole purpose of producing in the sequence of its various scenes a clear, beautiful and inspiring drama and a truthful impression of the development of the State of Indiana," noted Langdon.

These same ideas were used by local communities in developing their own pageants. The commission gave what help it could, securing centennial chairmen in all but three of Indiana's counties, with each responsible for selecting a county committee to plan the work. The plan worked. Director

Workers from the Indiana Bell Telephone Company prepare a float for a parade celebrating the state's centennial in Peru, Indiana, in August 1916. *Indiana Historical Society, P0248.*

Woodward reported that forty-five county or local pageants presented in 1916 were seen by an estimated 250,000 people, and anywhere from 30,000 to 40,000 Hoosiers participated in the performances.

Along with the weeklong pageant in Indianapolis, capital residents had the chance to hear from President Woodrow Wilson as part of activities for Centennial Highway Day on October 12, 1916. Invited to speak by Governor Ralston, who was a vigorous supporter of roadway improvements, Wilson arrived in the city by presidential train (which was late). While in Indianapolis, the president reviewed an automobile parade before delivering a speech on the need for good roads to ten thousand people at the Fairgrounds Coliseum.

Perhaps the commission's crowning achievement came with the development of Indiana's first state parks. The movement began in April 1915 when Governor Ralston received a letter from Juliet V. Strauss, a nationally known writer living in Rockville, Indiana, appealing for help in saving the Turkey Run area in Parke County from being sold to timber interests. The commission created a special parks committee with Richard Lieber, who would become the first director of the Indiana Department of Conservation, as chairman.

President Wilson, Gov. Ralston and Mayor Viewing parade from Monument

President Woodrow Wilson (*left*) waves his hat to the crowd at the Centennial Highway Day parade around Monument Circle, October 12, 1916. Joining Wilson on the reviewing stand were Governor Ralston (*center*) and Indianapolis mayor Joseph E. Bell (*right*). *Bass Photo Company Collection, Indiana Historical Society.*

While talks for purchasing the Turkey Run property for the state were underway, the commission learned of the opportunity to purchase the rugged area of McCormick's Creek in Owen County. A total of $5,250 was raised, one-fourth of which by Owen County residents, and McCormick's Creek became Indiana's first state park. The commission later acquired the Turkey Run property.

When the last notes of music from the various pageants faded away and celebrants packed their costumes, the commission attempted to take advantage of the new opportunities presented by the centennial observance. Although a 1917 bill calling for the establishment of a permanent state agency for history failed, the commission was resurrected following World War I to organize a county-by-county war history. Since that time, Indiana has consistently funded a state historical agency (today known as the Indiana Historical Bureau).

"OLD FAITHFUL" ON LAKE MICHIGAN

On March 19, 1861, the citizens of Michigan City, Indiana, learned that President Abraham Lincoln had decided to appoint a new keeper for what was then Indiana's only lighthouse on the Great Lakes. For an annual salary of $6,000, the new lighthouse keeper—a cousin of Schuyler Colfax, who was the *South Bend St. Joseph Valley Register* editor and later vice president under Ulysses S. Grant—faced the arduous task of twice-nightly trips to recharge the lamp with lard oil. In forty-three years on the job, the keeper faithfully kept the beacon lit, earning the title of "the sailor's true friend." The keeper's name was Harriet A. Colfax.

The Old Lighthouse Museum, which is operated by the Michigan City Historical Society, preserves the deeds of Colfax and others like her who helped guide sailors safely through the often-dangerous waters of Lake Michigan. Although the lighthouse, which was placed on the National Register of Historic Places in 1974, is no longer in operation, it still manages to shed light on the history of the city and life on the lake.

Dubbed "Old Faithful" by grateful sailors, the lighthouse was established in 1835 when Major Isaac C. Elston, the original purchaser of the land on which Michigan City was founded, deeded to the federal government a strip of land running from the bend of Trail Creek to Lake Michigan for the construction of a lighthouse. The first light, however, was not in a building but was instead a "postlight"—a lantern on top of a tall post—located about one hundred feet west of the present lighthouse.

A circa 1940 view of the U.S. government lighthouse in Michigan City, Indiana. The 1858 on the side of the building indicates the year the lighthouse was built. *Indiana Historical Society, P0411.*

Constructing a permanent structure proved to be a challenge. Although a $7,000 contract was let in 1836 for a forty-foot-high whitewashed lighthouse tower topped with a lantern and a keeper's dwelling, the contractors had to endure such hardships as the loss of building materials in a storm and funding delays. Unfortunately, because funds originally appropriated for the work were not used in that fiscal year, the monies had to be returned to the government. The funds were reappropriated, however, and the lighthouse was finally completed in 1837.

One witness described the finished product as "a story and a half house, plastered on the outside and dazzling in its whiteness, more of a portico than a veranda ornamented the front and was covered with trailing vines. It fronted south and was surrounded by a grove of small oaks on the west. The well-kept lawn was dotted with shrubbery, flowers, and enclosed by a low rustic fence, and from a little wicket gate led a white graveled walk to the residence. The light tower was a detached cone-shaped structure." The first lighthouse keeper, Edmund B. Harrison, was appointed on December 9, 1837, and received $350 per year for his efforts.

Twenty-one years after the lighthouse was completed, the federal government, spurred on by the need for a brighter light for the increased shipping traffic on the lake, built a new lighthouse using Joliet stone for the foundation and Milwaukee brick for the upper portion. The date of construction, 1858, was inscribed on the south wall. The lighthouse's north end contained a French-designed Fresnel lens, fueled by sperm oil, the light from which could be seen for fifteen miles.

A native of Ogdensburg, New York, Harriet Colfax came to Michigan City in 1853, reportedly to forget a failed romance. Before her appointment as lighthouse keeper, she worked as a typesetter for her brother, *Michigan City Gazette* publisher Richard Colfax, and also gave music lessons. She was aided in her lighthouse duties by Ann Hartwell, who taught school in Michigan City. Although described as having a petite figure "peculiarly unfitted for the position of lightkeeper," Colfax faithfully kept the light burning in spite of often adverse conditions.

In 1871, a small postlight was installed on the east pier and later was moved to the west pier. Colfax had the responsibility of keeping the beacon lit, even though she had to cross Trail Creek by boat to service the light. Patricia Harris, museum curator, described one particularly rough journey endured by Colfax:

Miss Colfax warmed the lard oil and started on her hazardous trip. Twice she was driven back before she gained the beacon, and when at last she reached it, she found to her dismay and annoyance that the lock had been tampered with and it would not open. In her desperation she finally broke a pane of glass, crawled through the opening and inserted the lamp in place. However, so much time had been lost that the oil had congealed and would not ignite. Lamp in hand, she started back to the lighthouse through an icy shower, slipped, fell, rose and slipped again, but finally reached the end of the pier in safety. The oil was again heated and again she started out for the beacon, this time accomplishing her task.

In addition to her usual chores as lighthouse keeper, Colfax dutifully kept journals that recorded such events as boat dockings, weather conditions, shipwrecks and lighthouse conditions. In one entry, Colfax noted that the lock of the beacon had been "tampered with by some parties who had not the fear of law before their eyes." Her last entry, upon her retirement in October 1904, read, "Fair, warm wind, smokey atmosphere. Received another call from Mr. [Thomas] Armstrong, my successor." She died five months later at the age of eighty.

Postcard showing ice and snow covering the pier leading to the lighthouse in Michigan City. *Indiana Historical Society, M0408.*

The federal government extensively renovated the lighthouse in 1904 by adding two rooms to each floor on the north side and creating duplex apartments. Workmen also removed the tower from the roof. The keeper and his family used all three floors on the east side, and the assistant keeper used those on the west. On October 20, 1904, the lantern was moved to a new fog-signal lighthouse at the entrance of Michigan City's harbor.

In 1933, the light in the harbor was electrified, and the keeper on shore could turn it on by simply flipping a switch. Six years later, the United States Coast Guard assumed responsibility for the light. Since the Coast Guard had its own station a short distance from the Old Lighthouse, it rented the structure as a private residence for a time; the building also served as home to the Coast Guard Auxiliary. The lighthouse gradually deteriorated before the government declared it surplus property in 1960.

The Government Services Administration sold the Old Lighthouse to the city in 1963 for $18,500. Two years later, the Michigan City Historical Society entered into a lease with the city to restore the facility and turn it into a museum within two years. However, it took eight years and approximately $100,000 to renovate the property. On June 9, 1973, the Old Lighthouse was officially dedicated and opened to the public.

THE FATHER OF INDIANA HISTORY AND THE LAKE MONSTER

On August 8, 1838, readers of the *Indiana Democrat* in Indianapolis were greeted by a special correspondence from the northern Indiana community of Logansport that had been originally printed in the *Logansport Telegraph*.

The article, signed "A Visiter to the Lake," reported on the sighting of a sixty-foot-long creature sliding through the once quiet waters of Lake Manitou, located near Rochester in what is now Fulton County. One eyewitness, who viewed the monster from the safety of the shoreline, described the beast's head as "being about three feet across the frontal bone…but the neck tapering, and having the character of the serpent; color dingy, with large bright yellow spots."

This was not the first time such a creature had made an appearance. The behemoth had loomed large in the legend of the Potawatomi Indians of the area, who called it "Meshekenabek." The Potawatomis' belief in the monster was so great that one local historian noted that "they would not hunt upon its borders, nor fish in its waters for fear of incurring the anger of the Evil spirit that made its home in this little woodland lake." In fact, the Potawatomis later cautioned white settlers against building a mill on the lake, predicting that the monster would "rush forth from his watery dominions and take indiscriminate vengeance on all those who resided near the sacred lake." The power of the tale was such that several men who worked in surveying the lake for the mill reported seeing the monster—making it difficult to find men willing to finish the job.

The monster inhabiting what came to be celebrated as "Devil's Lake" soon received the attention of newspapers not only in Indiana's capital city but also in such far-flung locales as Buffalo, Boston and New York. The creature's existence became hotly debated by Logansport's two newspapers—the *Telegraph*, which printed the first report of the monster in its July 21, 1838 edition, and its rival publication, the *Herald*, which lambasted the *Telegraph*'s story and touted instead the existence of another monster in Bass Lake. Other doubters scoffed at those who claimed to have seen the creature, saying that the "men saw the monster through glass, the glass of a whiskey jug."

The man responsible for the *Telegraph*'s publication of this unlikely story was a person who, in all other respects, seemed to be the least likely to come up with such a whopper of a tale: John Brown Dillon, who became known as the "Father of Indiana History" for his much-respected *History of Indiana*, which went through four editions between 1843 and 1859 and helped save future the state's past for future generations through his work with a number of early Hoosier historical organizations. His writings won praise from Indiana historians who came after him, with one, Emma Lou Thornbrough, commending Dillon for being the "only person in the state in this period whose writings deserved to be called history by modern standards of historical scholarship." Dillon had help in his "Devil's Lake" escapade, as noted pioneer Hoosier artist George Winter contributed a number of the articles about the monster printed in the *Telegraph* and an illustration featuring a method of possibly capturing the creature.

Details about Dillon's early life are sketchy at best. Born sometime in 1808 in Wellsburg, Brooke County, in what is now West Virginia, Dillon and his family soon moved to Belmont County, Ohio. After the death of his father, nine-year-old Dillon was apprenticed to a printer in Charleston. At the age of seventeen, Dillon moved to Cincinnati, where he displayed literary skill, having his poems published in several local newspapers. Sometime in his life, Dillon had suffered a visual malformity and always could be seen wearing dark-green eyeglasses equipped with side mirrors. His friend Horace P. Biddle, a Logansport attorney and later Indiana Supreme Court judge, recalled that "familiar as we were for so many years, meeting at all hours of the day, under all circumstances—even to bathing in the river—I never saw his face without his glasses on, which he always wore fastened by a little cord around the back of his head." After Dillon's death, when his body was being prepared for burial, Biddle investigated and discovered that his

John Brown Dillon, the "Father of Indiana History." *Indiana State Library.*

friend's "left eye had been broken, apparently by a blow of some kind, and partially wasted away."

By 1834, Dillon had settled in Logansport, where he studied law and was admitted to the Cass County bar in 1840. He never, however, established a law practice, preferring instead to spend his time on "hoary border legends, traditional story, but more especially local history," as Biddle noted. Dillon pursued these interests through a career in pioneer journalism, starting work as an editor for the *Logansport Canal Telegraph* in August 1834. A year later, he purchased an interest in the newspaper, which, by 1836, had changed its name to the *Logansport Telegraph*.

Described by his friends as shy, serious and intellectual in nature, Dillon exhibited another side to his character in an incident during his time as the *Telegraph*'s editor. Biddle recalled that he, Dillon and Winter were in his law office on April 1, 1840, when someone mentioned that it was April Fool's Day. Dillion was keen on the idea of fooling somebody; he wrote out a notice and tacked it on a billboard in the office of the hotel where he lived: "There will be exhibited at the court house this evening a living manthorp, from 8 to 10 o'clock. Sir Roger De Coverly, Manager."

Dillion's notice had an immediate effect. At dinner that night, Biddle recalled, clergymen, lawyers and other learned men of the community were searching every book they could find to learn what a manthorp was. "The word manthorp is really a compound of two Anglo-Saxon words," Biddle noted, "meaning 'the man of the village.' For a long time afterwards Mr. Dillon's 'April Fool' was locally a popular anecdote."

If the Lake Manitou monster is but a legend, then the "living manthrop" was not Dillon's first practical joke on the citizens of Logansport. The bespectacled editor, however, did not herald the monster's existence by himself. He had the assistance of the English-born Winter, who came to Logansport from Indianapolis in May 1837, as he later wrote, "for the purpose…of seeing and learning something of the Indians and exercising the pencil in that direction." Winter obviously had learned something of the Indians' "Devil's Lake" legend—knowledge he used for his articles in Dillon's *Telegraph*.

Later in life, Winter confirmed his authorship of some of the newspaper articles about the monster and expressed his surprise at the reception they had received. In a December 16, 1871 letter to B.J. Lossing, Winter wrote, "I felt a deep interest in this inland lake as I had gathered up the facts in relation to the Indian story associated with it.…From the peculiarity of the tradition and from its emanating from a 'Wild Region' of [the] country, it won the attention of the press and went 'the rounds' unexpectedly to my anticipation or aspirations."

Although Winter may have expressed astonishment over the response to his article years after the fact, initially he did try to stir up some reaction through the newspaper. The week following the first article on the creature, the *Telegraph* printed a second story, titled "The Monster." The story proposed calling a meeting to discuss the possibility of an expedition to the lake to "capture the Leviathan that inhabits its mysterious depths." Written by Winter, the article went on to sound a battle cry to the local citizenry:

> *It would be well, probably to suggest the propriety of those holding a meeting who are favorable, and willing to support the effort to ascertain with certainty, whether the mysterious, old and cherished tradition of the Indians, is based upon a KNOWN species of fish, or serpent, or whether the field of science shall be extended by the discovery of a new species of animal, peculiar to this beautiful and not oft visited Lake Mani-i-too.*
>
> *It is truly astonishing that such a small inland lake, so remote too from the seas, should be as mysterious in its depths as it is in its legendary associations. But so it is. Boys! Up with your harpoons and to the Lake Man-i-too. The weather, the season, the forest in all its leafy beauties offer you inducements to leave the turmoil of every day life for a week, and seek relaxation in the exciting expedition to the Devil's Lake.*

Although a meeting was organized on August 11, 1838, at the Eel River and Cass County Seminary to discuss methods of capturing the monster, no expedition to the lake was ever mounted by Logansport residents. According to a local historian, a "sickly season, combined with other circumstances," prevented the investigation from happening. The creature remained safe and hidden.

Articles on the monster inhabiting Lake Manitou died out from the *Telegraph*'s pages by September 1838. Interest in the creature was resurrected in 1849, however, when Winter wrote an article for the *Logansport Journal* on "The Monster Caught at Last." The story reported the capture of a fish weighing "several hundred weight—the head alone weighs upward of 30 pounds and its capacity for swallowing may be imagined when we state the mouth measures three feet in circumference." Also, in 1888, according to a history of Fulton County, a 116-pound spoonbill catfish was pulled from the lake by four men, who placed the fish in a horse trough by the courthouse in Rochester and charged people ten cents for a peek at the great beast. They later took their catch exhibit in Logansport. Eventually, they butchered the catfish and sold it at ten cents per pound.

Dillon's work as a historian soon usurped his journalism career. He started his research on a history of Indiana in 1838, receiving assistance from U.S. Senator John Tipton, a close friend. Dillon left Logansport in 1842, moving

The lake monster is out of sight in this view of boaters plying the waters of Lake Manitou, circa 1910. *Indiana Historical Society, M0408.*

to Indianapolis to pursue his historical studies and find funding for his history. Although he could rely on materials from the state library and private collections, Dillon lamented that "many interesting facts, connected with the early settlement of Indiana, have been perverted, or lost forever, because they were never recorded, and the stream of tradition seldom bears to the present, faithfully, the history of the past." His *Historical Notes on the Discovery and Settlement of the Territory Northwest of the Ohio* appeared in 1843 and was followed sixteen years later by his *History of Indiana.* His posthumously published *Oddities of Colonial Legislation in America* came out in 1879.

Fellow Hoosier historian George S. Cottman, founder of the *Indiana Magazine of History,* dubbed Dillon as the "Father of Indiana History" and praised him as the first in the state to enter the field "with any seriousness of purpose, and his contributions exceed in value any that have come after." In his writing, Dillon displayed "immense industry, unflagging perseverance and an ever-present purpose to find and state the truth," said Cottman.

Dillon himself wrote that in his work he was striving to give an "impartial" recording of history. He noted in his preface to his *History of Indiana* that in writing the book, he attempted to keep his mind free from such influences as "ambitious contentions between distinguished men, or from false traditions, or from national partialities and antipathies, or from excited conflicts between the partisans of antagonistic political systems, or from dissensions among uncharitable teachers of different creeds of religion."

In 1845, the state legislature elected Dillon as state librarian, a post he held until 1851, when a Democratic legislature replaced him with Nathaniel Bolton. Dillon later served as assistant secretary of state and secretary to the State Board of Agriculture and held numerous offices with the Indiana Historical Society, including secretary and librarian. He proved indefatigable at adding books and manuscripts to the society's early collection. In addition to state offices, Dillon served on a variety of Indianapolis governmental bodies, including being a member of the Marion County Library Board and a school trustee.

In 1862, Dillon left Indianapolis for Washington, D.C., where he received a position as clerk to the Department of the Interior, later moving to a job as clerk with the House Military Affairs Committee. Civic leaders in Indianapolis remembered Dillon's contributions to the state, with noted attorney Calvin Fletcher calling on the state legislature to bring the historian back to Indiana to write a history of the state's contribution to the Civil War. Dillon finally returned to Indianapolis in 1875, living in a room at Johnson's Building on Washington Street. He struggled to make a living, even having to sell his beloved library to make ends meet. Dillon died at age seventy-one and was buried at Crown Hill Cemetery.

AMELIA EARHART AT PURDUE UNIVERSITY

In his twenty-three years as Purdue University's president, Dr. Edward Charles Elliott made many changes to the West Lafayette campus, making it one of the country's leading technical and engineering institutions. As the university's leader, Elliott operated under what he called "a doctrine of chance." He noted that "chance meetings, unexpected conversations, all play a more important part of an individual's life than do most planned and carefully executed experiences."

One of the "chance meetings" Elliott described resulted in a major coup for Purdue when, in June 1935, the president announced the appointment of a visiting faculty member as a career counselor for the university's female students. The new addition to the staff had already achieved worldwide fame but passed into legend following her stint at the Hoosier school. Purdue had landed Amelia Earhart.

Although Earhart—dubbed "Lady Lindy" for both her resemblance to Charles Lindbergh and her accomplishments as a flier in the 1920s and 1930s—spent only a short time at Purdue, both she and the university benefited from the relationship. Along with the mountains of publicity garnered from her presence on the faculty, Purdue also became the beneficiary of Earhart's person-to-person talents as she encouraged female students to embark on careers normally reserved for men.

In Earhart's case, her husband, George P. Putnam, convinced Elliott and the university to help fund a "flying laboratory" for his wife's use. Through the Purdue University Research Foundation and donations from

Amelia Earhart noted that the time to worry came "three months before a flight. Decide then whether or not the goal is worth the risks involved. If it is, stop worrying. To worry is to add another hazard." *Purdue University Libraries, Karnes Archives and Special Collections.*

Earhart sits atop her Lockheed Electra aircraft, with Purdue University coeds lined up along one side, September 20, 1936. The women are, *left to right*, Virginia Gardener, Rufina Sexton, Babara Sweeney, Betty Spilman, Barbara Cook, Louis Schickler, Mary Johnston, Mary L. Hinchman, Dorothy Hewitt and Gaby D. Roe. *Purdue University Libraries, Karnes Archives and Special Collections.*

Hoosier businessmen David Ross, J.K. Lilly Sr. and others, the university established in April 1936 an Amelia Earhart Fund for Aeronautical Research that aided the aviatrix in purchasing the twin-motored Lockheed Electra airplane Earhart would use on her ill-fated "Round-the-World" flight from which she vanished in July 1937.

Already famous for her daring aerial exploits, including being the first woman passenger on a transatlantic flight and the first woman to fly solo across the Atlantic Ocean, Earhart and Purdue's paths first crossed in September 1934, when she addressed the fourth annual "Women and the Changing World" conference sponsored by the *New York Herald Tribune*. Present at the conference to speak about "New Frontiers for Youth," Elliott stayed to hear Earhart's remarks on aviation's future and the role women might play in its advancement.

Intrigued by the flier's speech, Elliott arranged a meeting with Earhart and Putnam. A born promoter and a person who regularly hobnobbed with America's elite, Putnam was immediately impressed with Elliott's style. "He is a lean, powerful man who combines the brisk attributes of a dynamo with the important qualities of scholarship and human vision. He has a habit of referring to himself with humorous depreciation, as just a Hoosier schoolmaster, but no gentleman from Indiana ever knew his way about more competently than he," said Putnam.

After the trio dined at the Coffee House Club in New York, Elliott came straight to the point. According to Putnam's version of the meeting, Elliott told Earhart, "We want you at Purdue." Earhart expressed little surprise at the offer, merely replying, "I'd like that if it can be arranged. What would you think I should do?" The university president replied that he envisioned Earhart's role as passing along to Purdue's nearly eight hundred female students "the inspirational opportunities" open to them in America's changing society. "I think you could supply some spark which would help to take up the lag between the swift eddying of the world around modern women and the tardier echoes of the schoolroom," Elliott remarked to Earhart.

With the offer made, the three spent the next two hours developing the idea into a workable plan. With her busy schedule, Earhart could not be a full-time faculty member at Purdue but would attempt to spend at least a month at the university during the school year as a career consultant for women. For her efforts, she would receive from Purdue a $2,000 salary. Along with guiding women students toward new careers, she also served as a technical adviser in aeronautics to Purdue, which was, at that time, the only university in the country equipped with its own airport.

To Earhart, however, the "problems and opportunities of these girls [at Purdue] were quite as much my concern as aviation matters" when she agreed to take the job. Writing about her time at the university in her posthumously published book, *Last Flight*, Earhart admitted that she had "something of a chip on my shoulder when it comes to modern feminine education." She noted that women, especially those whose tastes are outside the normal routine, often did not get a fair chance to develop their talents. "I have known girls who should be tinkering with mechanical things instead of making dresses, and boys who would do better at cooking than engineering." Purdue, which she called "my kind of school, a technical school where all instruction has practicality," offered her a chance to test those beliefs.

In announcing Earhart's appointment on June 2, 1935, Elliott termed her acceptance as "gratifying to the university and significant to education."

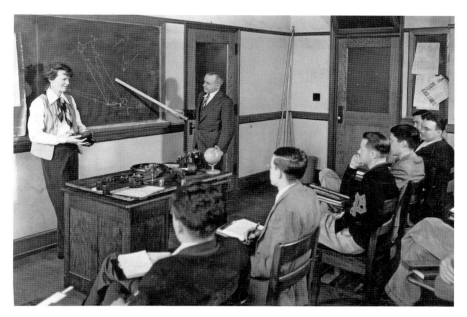

Earhart assists Captain G.W. Haskins teach a class in aerial navigation to aerodynamics students at the Purdue University Airport, April 20, 1936. *Purdue University Libraries, Karnes Archives and Special Collections.*

Emphasizing the flier's interest in educating women for the future, he added that Earhart represented "better than any young woman of this generation the spirit and the courageous skill of what may be called the new pioneering. At no other point in our educational system is there greater need for courageous pioneering and constructive planning than woman's education." Earhart, "a creative artist in the great art of human adventure," the Purdue scholar believed, could help the university successfully attack the "most important modern unsolved problem of higher education—the effective education of young women."

Earhart, fresh from a lecture tour that saw her give twenty-nine speeches in one month, arrived on Purdue's West Lafayette campus to assume her duties on November 6, 1935. The *Lafayette Journal and Courier* heralded the famous flier's arrival in Indiana with a page-one headline declaring "Amelia Earhart Leaves Air to Guide Purdue Girls in Careers." With Earhart scheduled to be at the university only three weeks, the newspaper noted that she would "have little opportunity for leisure during her sojourn on the campus."

The reporter's prediction quickly came to pass. In her first few days at Purdue, Earhart attended a luncheon for the home economics department, served as guest of honor at a Mortar Board luncheon, met the student body at an afternoon tea in the Memorial Union building and spoke at a special convocation at the Memorial gymnasium.

Given workspace in the dean of women's office and living in South Hall, Earhart became a familiar sight on campus. Students flocked to the flier's side, especially at dinnertime, and tried not only to imitate her style of dress (which was casual, to say the least) but her mannerisms as well. "These were the days when table manners were considered somewhat important," noted Helen Schleman, in charge of the dormitory where Earhart stayed. "Amelia's posture at table, when she was deep in conversation, was apt to be sitting forward on the edge of her chair—both elbows on the table—and chin cupped in hands. Naturally, the question was 'If Miss Earhart can do it why can't we?' The stock reply was 'As soon as you fly the Atlantic, you may!'"

Earhart managed to fit in well with dormitory life at Purdue. Marian Frazier, who lived in the same dorm as the flier, remembered that it seemed as though Earhart was always "terribly busy," noting that she heard Earhart working away at her typewriter as late as midnight. Frazier also recalled studying one night when Earhart suddenly appeared and asked to borrow a pen for a short time. The excited Frazier could not keep the news to herself, so when her celebrity neighbor returned the borrowed pen, she was greeted by a roomful of coeds, all wanting to catch a glimpse of the celebrated pilot.

The flier's casual style and dress (slacks instead of skirts) became the envy of Purdue's coeds and raised others' eyebrows. Robert Topping, in his history of the university, reported that some faculty wives—the "local guardians of mores and morals in the conservative 1930s atmosphere of West Lafayette"—were scandalized by one incident when Earhart, dressed in her usual slacks, went into town one afternoon and visited Bartlett's Drug Store. Not only did Earhart have the temerity to wear improper clothing, she further shocked the wives by sitting (unescorted by a man) at a stool, ordering a soda and smoking a cigarette. "Such hussy behavior was barely tolerable in a conservative campus town," Topping wrote.

Along with facing the faculty wives' wrath, Earhart also had to endure questions from some faculty members about whether she was qualified for her job. A.A. Potter, Purdue's dean of engineering, said that he did not think Earhart belonged at the university because she lacked the proper education (although she had enrolled at Columbia University as a premed student, she never graduated). Acknowledging Earhart's courage, Potter nevertheless told a reporter that the flier "had too poor an educational foundation to utilize her courage and that was her disadvantage." Another faculty member, a woman, had an answer ready for Potter: "The dean is a scholar and he doesn't understand that you have to motivate kids before you can get them to be scholars."

Despite these challenges, Earhart stuck to her main task: counseling Purdue's women students about potential careers. Toward that end, she prepared a questionnaire seeking answers from them about such issues as why they were in college, if they wanted a career, how marriage might affect their choices and what part a husband might play in their life. Of those responding to the questionnaire, Earhart found that approximately 92 percent indicated that they wanted a career. According to Putnam, his wife wanted to find out about the student's after-college plans to help university officials in reconstructing courses so that they might be more beneficial. "She thought too that such exploration might help the students themselves to clarify their own thinking, to agree with themselves on a general objective, perhaps even a specific one," Putnam noted.

Earhart discussed with Purdue administrators the possibility of creating a "household engineering" course for those women who wanted to remain homemakers. "Many a stay-at-home girl," said Earhart, "would welcome practical training in what to do when the doorbell fails to function, the plumbing clogs…and the thousand-and-one other mechanical indispositions that can occur about the house, often easily enough fixed if one has rudimentary knowledge how to fix them." Disliking discrimination between men's work and women's work, she also pointed out the need for male students to gather some experience in homemaking, noting that most men "enter into marriage with little training in domestic economy, know little about food and how it should be prepared, little about child training and their duties as parents. What, I wonder, is going to be done about all that."

In her personal dealings with student, Earhart, using her own experiences as a trendsetter, painted no rosy picture of instant acceptance for women entering new careers. Marguerite Coll, who studied electrical engineering at Purdue, recalled Earhart clearly explaining to her and two other female students "what some of the obstacles are in the way of women who want to go into what's always been known as a man's field. She was encouraging though. She didn't see why, if a woman had special talents along that line, she couldn't go out and show 'em!"

That kind of advice worried some people. According to Putnam, one Purdue professor declared that if Earhart kept on encouraging the university's coeds to pursue careers, they "won't be willing to get married

Earhart helps horticulture students Ruth Shelburne and Howard Emme with some plants. *Purdue University Libraries, Karnes Archives and Special Collections.*

and lead the quiet life for which Nature intended them." In one regard, the male professor might have been right. As an unidentified female student proclaimed after Earhart's stay at the university had ended, "No one ever pepped us up so."

Talking with students, Earhart developed what she called "surface impressions" about the university that she shared with the school's administrators. She noted that there appeared to exist at Purdue rigid boundary lines between different disciplines. "It seems to me there should be much more interchange of instructors and subjects between these, which would lead to the education of people rather than to the selected specimens numbered and tagged Home Ec[onomics] or EE [Electrical Engineering] or what-not," said Earhart. She added that lowering the walls between schools might help eliminate the "condescending attitude" on the part of male students toward their female counterparts. "Today," said Earhart, "it is almost as if the subjects themselves had sex so firm is the line drawn between what girls and boys should study."

Although she spent only a short time at the university, Earhart's ties to Purdue played a key role in securing for her the money and equipment necessary for attempting what became her final flight. On April 19, 1936, the university announced the establishment of the Amelia Earhart Fund for Aeronautical Research, made possible by the Purdue Research Foundation. With contributions totaling $50,000 from such philanthropists as J.K. Lilly Sr. and David Ross, and later donations of cash and equipment from such companies as Western Electric, Goodyear and Goodrich, Earhart purchased a "flying laboratory"—a twin-motored, ten-passenger Lockheed Electra aircraft. The plane, built in Burbank, California, included such special features as extra gasoline tanks for extended flight, an automatic pilot and a two-way radio.

The announcement received nationwide attention, as newspapers from New York to Los Angeles trumpeted Earhart's "flying laboratory." Noting that "aviation is a business to me and my ambition is that the project shall provide practical results," Earhart first planned to use the plane for a year to gather research material on such areas as speed and fuel consumption, oxygen use, radio communication and navigation and the effect of prolonged flight on humans. After completing her research, Earhart then hoped to make an "interesting" flight in the all-metal Electra. "But circumstances," she noted, "made it appear wise to postpone the research and attempt the flight first."

The flight Earhart so offhandedly mentioned turned into a monumental undertaking: an attempt to become the first woman to fly around the world. Once that feat had been accomplished, the plane would become the Purdue Research Foundation's property. Royalties from a book Earhart expected to write about the experience and moneys from exhibiting the aircraft were to have been used by the foundation to further pure and applied scientific research in aeronautics. As preparations for the flight were being made, Earhart was asked time and time again why she had decided to attempt the flight. Her answer came right to the point: "Because I want to." She called the trip a "shining adventure, beckoning with new experiences, added knowledge of flying, of peoples—of myself." Also, Earhart noted that with the flight behind her, she would become more useful to herself and to the aeronautical program at Purdue.

On June 1, 1937, Earhart and her navigator, Fred Noonan, took off from Miami, Florida, in the Electra on the first leg of a planned around-the-world flight. The trip proceeded smoothly until the difficult 2,570-mile flight from Lae, New Guinea, to Howland Island. The two never reached their destination. In spite of a massive search, no trace could then be found of the plane and its crew. On the day she disappeared, Earhart had been scheduled to deliver a lecture at Purdue on the subject "What Next in the Air?" Two

Seen here in the cockpit of her Lockheed Electra aircraft, Earhart wrote to her husband before her ill-fated flight that she was aware of the hazards but that women had to "try to do things as men have tried. When they fail, their failure must be a challenge to others." *Library of Congress.*

weeks after Earhart disappeared, Elliott telegraphed Putnam the following message: "George, she would not want us to grieve or weep; she would have been a heroine in any age."

Although Purdue's investment had crashed somewhere in the Pacific Ocean, the university received tangible benefits from its association with Earhart, including nationwide publicity. Also, Purdue's female students had a unique opportunity to interact with a person who typified women's changing role in modern society. As for Earhart, her time at the Hoosier university offered her a chance to test her skills as both a pilot and an educator. Looking back at that short period in Earhart's career, Putnam said that her job at Purdue provided her with "one of the most satisfying adventures of her life."

"NOBODY WANTED US"

BLACK AVIATORS AT FREEMAN FIELD

I n January 1945, the American effort in World War II was reaching a climax. GIs in Europe had turned back the last German offensive on the Western Front at the Battle of the Bulge, and in the Pacific Theater, U.S. troops were recapturing the Philippines from the Japanese. While military operations were reaching a fever pitch overseas, back home in Indiana activity was winding down at a military installation that had awarded wings to approximately four thousand airmen: Freeman Field, located near Seymour.

Although the U.S. War Department had placed Freeman Field on an inactive basis on January 27, 1945, the air base soon became a proving ground in a different struggle—not against fascism on the battlefront, but against racism on the homefront.

Denied access to the base's officers' club on account of their race, about sixty officers from the all-black 477th Bombardment Group, which was receiving bomber training at Freeman Field, were arrested on April 3, 1945, when they attempted to enter what the *Indianapolis Recorder* referred to as a "swanky and modern officers club set up by the outfit." After the dust had settled, three officers—Roger C. Terry and Marsden A. Thompson, both of Los Angeles, California, and Shirley R. Clinton of Camden, New Jersey—faced a court-martial, and nearly one hundred men from the air group were jailed at Godman Field in Kentucky.

The calm atmosphere of a small Civil Aeronautics Administration emergency field located southwest of Seymour changed following the

Japanese attack on the American base at Pearl Harbor in the Hawaiian Islands, plunging the United States into World War II. On May 6, 1942, the War Department announced that the Seymour CAA Field had been selected as a site for an advanced aerial training center for bomber pilots, to be designated as Seymour Army Airfield. The base, renamed Freeman Army Airfield on March 3, 1943, in honor of the late Captain Richard S. Freeman of Winamac, Indiana, included more than four hundred buildings and was built at a cost of $15 million. The 2,550-acre facility the federal government created in Jackson County was "the epitome of military airfield design," according to Louis Osterman's 1986 history of the base. The installation had an immediate positive financial impact on a community still reeling from the Great Depression.

Officially activated on December 1, 1942, under the command of Colonel Elmer T. Rundquist, the base welcomed its first group of soldiers just seven

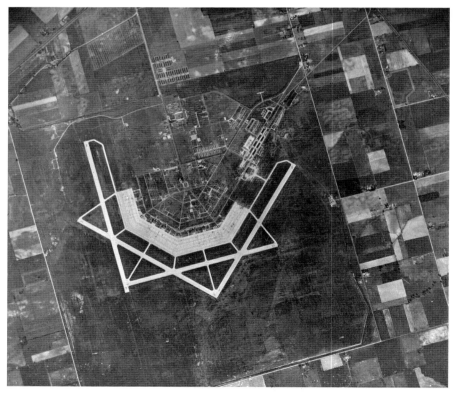

A 1950s aerial view of Freeman Field in Seymour, Indiana, a former air base during World War II. The field was turned over to the city in 1947. *Indiana Historical Society, P0411.*

days later. The added population proved to be a boon for area businesses. "The stores were open on Saturday night then, and the sidewalks were packed from curb to store with townspeople, the farmers of the area and their families, and soldiers in their wool, khaki uniforms and jaunty overseas caps," Seymour resident Carolyn Mahon told Osterman.

To help meet the soldiers' recreational needs, the city had been planning, even before the first troops reached the base, to open a United Service Organizations center. City officials organized a USO Council and obtained the use of the former Greeman Furniture Store. The club opened in December 1942 and was the scene of several dances and other activities for soldiers. The club, however, did not provide services to *all* military personnel stationed at the base. On January 21, 1943, the first members of the black 320th Aviation Squadron arrived at the Seymour field. The nearly six hundred squadron members were used primarily as service troops, performing such duties as cooking in the mess hall and tending the base's twenty-acre garden.

Segregation was widespread in the armed forces during World War II. In fact, it was not until January 1941, after pressure from the National Association for the Advancement of Colored People and other groups, that the U.S. Army Air Forces allowed blacks to become pilots. After being threatened with a lawsuit, the War Department established an air unit (later designated as the 99th Pursuit Squadron) for African Americans near the Tuskegee Institute in Alabama. The Tuskegee Army Air Field, however, was completely segregated at the outset, with fliers commanded and trained by white officers.

Opportunities for blacks in the Hoosier State at the start of the war were little better than those offered by the military. "It was nearly impossible to find in Indiana a public place, institution, or group where whites accorded blacks an equal and open reception," historian James H. Madison noted in his history of the state from 1920 to 1945. Although there were no actual statutes on the books, in many communities black citizens encountered so-called sundown laws, forbidding them from staying in the city after dark. In most aspects of their daily lives, from eating in restaurants to attending movies, African American Hoosiers faced discrimination and segregation.

Jackson County was no different from any other Indiana community in the 1940s "in that segregation and insensitivity to civil rights issues were accepted facts of life," Osterman noted. Because black troops stationed at the airfield could not use the white USO club in Seymour, the USO Council established a separate facility for them on West Tipton Street, which was dedicated on February 14, 1943, in ceremonies held inside the center because of severe weather. Reverend John L. Prentice, Jackson County USO Council chairman, formally presented the club to the city "as a channel of service for the citizens."

Segregation continued to be a problem for the next black troops stationed at Freeman Field, the 477th Bombardment Group, which was part of the First Air Force. Under the command of a white officer, Colonel Robert Selway, a West Point graduate and Far East veteran, the unit "had traveled a rocky road since its activation in January 1944," according to Colonel Benjamin O. Davis Jr. As the first black graduate of the U.S. Military Academy in the twentieth century and a member of the famed Tuskegee Airmen, Davis took charge of the 477th during the height of the Freeman Field controversy.

The first black squadron to be trained in multiengine aircraft, the 477th had been originally stationed at Selfridge Field, located near Detroit. The field had a history of racial conflict. On January 1, 1944, some black officers who had attempted to enter the base's officers' club were blocked from doing so by the field's commander, Colonel William L. Boyd, and another white officer. The refusal of service flew in the face of the armed force's own rules, specifically Army Regulation 210-10. According to the regulation, officers' clubs and other social organizations were mandated to offer "all officers on duty at the post the right to full membership, either permanently or temporary." Alan Osur, who studied race relations in the AAF during World War II, found, however, that the military had "dogmatically pursued a system of segregation that was almost impossible to maintain. It even went so far as to violate War Department regulations in order to prevent the mixing of whites and blacks in officers' clubs."

Afraid that black "agitators" in the Detroit area might incite trouble with the airmen at Selfridge Field (race riots had broken out in the city in June 1943), the AAF moved the 477th to Godman Field near Fort Knox, Kentucky. At the new airfield, black officers were able to enjoy the full use of the officers' club. Racial relations, however, were not as harmonious as they seemed. While black servicemembers used the officers' club at Godman, their white supervisors used the facilities at the segregated Fort Knox. Osur pointed out that black airmen were powerless to protest the situation; since they were not assigned to Fort Knox, they could not use the facilities there.

Other problems plagued the black fliers at the Kentucky AAF base. Along with bad flying weather during the winter, the field suffered from a lack of proper hangar and apron space and the absence of an air-to-ground gunnery range. On March 1, 1945, the 477th moved from Godman to Freeman Field. Trouble, however, soon broke out between blacks and whites. The difficulties were not with Seymour residents, who, according to Captain Earl D. Lyon in his study of the bombardment group's war service, "were less openly antagonistic" to black officers than residents of similar small towns located near army airfields. Instead, the racial trouble broke out on the base about a familiar issue: the officers' club.

In attempting to keep black and white officers from using the same facilities, Selway, with the support of Major General Frank Hunter, took advantage of a loophole in army regulations by designating one officers' club at Freeman for supervisory personnel and a second one for trainees. The issue came to a head on the night of April 5, 1945, when nineteen black officers, disregarding an assistant provost marshal's order to stay out, entered the whites-only club. Shortly thereafter, two other groups of African Americans totaling seventeen officers joined the original group; all thirty-six were placed under arrest by the provost marshal. The next day, an additional twenty-one black officers were arrested when they tried to enter the club.

Through its public relations office, the command at Freeman Field attempted to place its own spin on the issue. It released a statement to the *Seymour Daily Tribune* to the effect that in the case of recreational facilities, it had "been a long standing policy which applies throughout the United States which maintains that it is unwise to have personnel in training utilizing the same recreational facilities with those who train them." Although the two groups might use the same instructional facilities—classrooms, training equipment, airplanes and so on—after normal duty hours "each…selects its own recreation and entertainment separately, on order that they may relax from their official status."

Despite the air base's best efforts, the outcry about the incident did not die down. First Air Force legal officers were soon on their way to Freeman Field to investigate the incident. They found that Selway's original order was "inexact and ambiguous as to its meaning or purpose," and all but three of the black officers were released (Clinton, Terry and Thompson remained under lock and key for allegedly pushing the provost marshal when they entered the club). A new directive from base commander Selway, however, sparked more protests and resulted in even more arrests.

Selway, with Hunter's assistance, drafted an order for black officers to sign outlining what facilities different personnel could use on the base. The directive also included a place for black officers' signatures indicating that they had read and fully understood the order. Even when that designation was stricken from the order and the black officers were asked merely to signify that they had read it, some continued to defy the authorities. A total

Arrested African American officers at Freeman Field await transportation to Godman Field in Kentucky following their protest. *Everett Collection Historical/Alamy Stock Photo.*

of 101 black servicemen—who became known as the 101 Club—refused to sign and were flown to Godman Field and placed under arrest awaiting court-martial.

Quentin P. Smith, who grew up in East Chicago, Indiana, and learned to fly while living there, was one of the 101 black officers arrested for refusing to sign the order. An Indiana State University graduate and former flying instructor at Tuskegee Institute, Smith, due to his large size, had to transfer from fighter aircraft to bomber duty. First Lieutenant Smith and the other black aviators did not receive a warm welcome when they arrived at Freeman Field. Smith remembered that Selway informed the group that, along with the officers' club, the base's tennis court and swimming pool were also off limits to them. The airmen did not greet the announcement favorably. "We booed the colonel loud and long," Smith recalled.

The Hoosier native had a more direct confrontation with his white commanding officer after the officers' club incident. Called into Selway's office and asked to sign the new directive, Smith replied in a clear voice,

Colonel Benjamin O. Davis stands in front of his P-51 Mustang fighter at an air base in Italy in March 1945. *Tony Frissell Collection, Library of Congress.*

"No, sir." Even when threatened by the colonel with Article 64, stating that failure to obey a superior officer's direct order could result in the death penalty, Smith stood firm.

Organizations throughout the United States, including the NAACP and black newspapers, swung into action on the officers' behalf. The War Department received several letters of concern from lawmakers, including U.S. Senator Arthur H. Vandenberg from Michigan, Congressman Adam Clayton Powell from New York and Congressman Louis Ludlow from Indiana. Congresswoman Helen Gahagan from California even telegraphed Secretary of War Henry L. Stimson urging that the officers be released. All these efforts paid off; in mid-April, charges against the 101 black airmen were dropped and they were freed.

Charges against the three officers accused of pushing the provost marshal, however, remained. By the time the three came to trial, the 477th had a new commander, Colonel Davis, former leader of the black 332nd Fighter Group. An all-black court-martial acquitted Thompson and Clinton of all charges, convicting only Terry for "offering violence against a superior officer." He received a $150 fine.

The Freeman Field situation deeply troubled Davis. Although he could understand the underlying feelings of prejudice shown by white officers from the Deep South, he could not understand "putting the issue of segregated facilities ahead of the need to prepare the group for war; nor the decision to move the 477th from one airfield to another, which halted progress toward combat readiness for several months." The 477th never had an opportunity to prove itself in combat, as the group was still at Godman Field when the Japanese surrendered to the Allies on August 14, 1945.

Although Freeman Field was placed on the inactive basis shortly after the officers' club fiasco, its role in America's war effort had not ended. In June 1945, the War Department selected the base to serve as a testing ground for captured enemy aircraft. Once again airplanes filled the skies over Seymour. Two years later, the War Assets Administration gave the facility to Seymour, which used the base as a municipal airport.

Freeman Field played a crucial role in training aircrews for combat, but its greatest contribution to America's fight against fascism was the incident with the black officers, which, as Osterman pointed out, "caught the attention of the military and forced a re-thinking of its policy of segregation." That policy, however, remained in place for a few more years after the war ended. In July 1948, President Harry Truman issued Executive Order 8891 mandating the armed forces to integrate. Truman's order could not instantly strip away the legacy left by the years of discrimination in the military. Perhaps reflecting the feelings of the hundreds of thousands of black troops who battled prejudice during World War II, Smith lamented, "Nobody wanted us."

THE OTHER HOOSIER POET

WILLIAM HERSCHELL

After waking one day in May 1919 at his home at 958 Tecumseh Place near Woodruff Place in Indianapolis, a longtime feature reporter for the *Indianapolis News* trudged wearily to breakfast. Turning to his wife, Josephine, the journalist complained that he had no idea what to write about for that day's issue. Unsure of what to do, he picked up his typewriter and traveled out of town, finally ending his sojourn in the countryside at Brandywine Creek in Greenfield, Indiana. At the creek, he spied an older man fishing while sitting on a log. When the reporter commented on the area's beauty, the fisherman responded, "I can't complain, after all God's been pretty good to Indiana, ain't he?"

The offhand remark on this lonely stretch of water inspired the reporter, William Herschell, to write his masterpiece, "Ain't God Good to Indiana?" The poem proved popular not only with Hoosiers (the work is inscribed on a bronze plaque in the rotunda of the Indiana Statehouse) but also with readers from around the country, who clamored for copies. The demand grew so great that Herschell's wife had to issue special printed facsimiles of the poem.

During his career at the *News*, which started in 1902 and ended with his death at age sixty-six in 1939, Herschell contributed countless poems and feature articles for the newspaper's Saturday edition. In addition, his World War I song "Long Boy" contributed the doughboy refrain, "Goodbye Ma! Goodbye Pa! Goodbye mule with your old heehaw!" to the nation's vocabulary. Herschell, a close companion of famed Hoosier poet James

Contemporary Indiana poet Jared Carter described William Herschell as a skilled writer whose poems employed every poetic device practical to "make them smooth, readable, legible and lots of fun." *Bass Photo Company Collection, Indiana Historical Society.*

Whitcomb Riley, worked in a corner of the newspaper's ninth floor that came to be known as the "Idle Ward." Along with Herschell, other members of that delightful company included cartoonists Gaar Williams and Frank McKinney "Kin" Hubbard, creator of the renowned cracker-barrel philosopher Abe Martin. The three men were all quite productive when it came to producing copy and illustrations, but they seemed idle to other newspaper employees because they always seemed to be able to find time to discuss and gossip about the issues of the day.

Born in Spencer, Indiana, on November 17, 1873, Herschell was the eldest of six children born to Scottish immigrants John and Martha (Leitch) Herschell. Trained as a blacksmith in his native Scotland, John worked for the Indianapolis and Vincennes Railroad and later served as foreman for a quarry near Spencer that supplied limestone for the state capitol in Indianapolis. One of William's earliest memories involved his father sitting by lamplight to recite to his family the poetry of Robert Burns. John's work with the Evansville, Rockport and Eastern Railroad took him and his family to a succession of communities in southwestern Indiana, including Rockport, Evansville, Huntingburg and Princeton.

Although at best an unfocused student, Herschell did display some of the writing talent he later used during his newspaper career. While in the

Huntingburg school system, he was falsely accused of running away with the teacher's pet dog. An unabashed Herschell penned the following in reply: "Teacher says I stole his dog / But why should I steal Jim, / When teachers with me all day long / And I can look at him?" Herschell's talent for thumbing his nose at the school's authorities proved to be his undoing.

As a seventh grader, Herschell, already a solid supporter of the Republican Party, played hooky from school to carry in a political parade a banner that proclaimed, "A Vote for [Grover] Cleveland Means Souphouses." The school's principal found out about Herschell's truancy—and political persuasion—and expelled him from school, noting, "Inasmuch as William Herschell had gone into politics he could not possibly wish further education."

With the assistance of his father, Herschell found work as an apprentice railroad machinist. In 1894, when Eugene Debs's American Railway Union told its members to refuse to handle Pullman cars in support of striking workers at the Pullman plants in Illinois, Herschell allied himself closely with the union cause. With the strike's failure, Herschell found himself out of a job. Leaving the Hoosier State, Herschell toiled at a succession of jobs, including stints in Chicago, Buffalo and Canada. Returning to the United States, he worked at an electric light plant in North Tonawanda, New York. He eventually found his way back to his native state, where he worked as a night machinist for the Monon Railroad.

On a visit to his family in Princeton in 1896, Herschell met James McCormick, who just three years before had started the *Princeton Evening News*, an independent Republican Party daily. McCormick offered Herschell a job, telling him, "I'll give you $9 a week, if you can get it." Herschell did not discover what his editor had meant until the end of his first week at the newspaper. After everyone else on the paper had received his wages, there remained only four dollars left for Herschell. Week after week, there never seemed to be enough funds to pay Herschell his full salary. On one occasion, McCormick even had to borrow brown wrapping paper from a local butcher to publish his afternoon newspaper. An editorial dedicated the issue as "A Souvenir Edition to Our Creditors." To supplement his meager income, Herschell served as the Princeton correspondent for several larger newspapers, including the *Indianapolis News*. Herschell sometimes used his money from other publications to buy enough newsprint for McCormick to print his paper.

Although McCormick and Herschell became close friends, the publisher did not stand in his protégé's way when, in 1898, Herschell received a job offer from the *Evansville Journal*. Before Herschell left for his new duties, he found waiting for him in the newspaper's editorial office a gold watch—a going-away present from McCormick. Later, Herschell dedicated his 1922 book *Howdy All: And Other Care-Free Rhymes* to McCormick, noting that the editor taught him it was "easier to swing a pencil than a hammer." A year after starting at the Evansville newspaper, Herschell left to join the staff of the *Indianapolis Press* as a police reporter. With the folding of the *Press* after only sixteen months, Herschell moved to the *Terre Haute Tribune*. He returned to Indianapolis in 1902 for a position with the *Indianapolis Journal*. Herschell's work at the *Journal* soon caught the attention of Dick Herrick, secretary to *Indianapolis News* editor Hilton U. Brown. Herrick told his boss that Herschell was "full of fun, can write rhymes and can make the dullest story read like a novel. He belongs here and ought to make a top feature man." Taking his secretary's advice, Brown hired Herschell in April 1902, beginning the reporter's thirty-seven-year association with the newspaper.

In his early years on the *News*, Herschell served as a police and court reporter and won the lasting respect of the Indianapolis Police Department. At slack times, members of the department and local media conducted mock trials at an old bicycle barn. Conducted by the newspapermen, these trials often concluded with the officers having to pay a cigar or two in fines. Herschell presided over the proceedings as judge. His wife, Josephine, who also worked at the *News*, noted that her husband acted like "a regular roughneck when he came home at night after hanging around the police station all day. But he changed a lot after he became a feature writer." Josephine also noted that her husband used to jokingly scold a clock that he had been given as a boy, especially when he arrived home at a later time than he had told her to expect him. "We had a lovely life together," she said.

In 1911, *News* editor Richard Smith, impressed with Herschell's poetry, assigned him to write poems and feature articles for the newspaper's Saturday edition. Herschell's poems about such staples of city life as policemen, firemen, street urchins and other characters appeared in a series titled "Songs of the City Streets." Later, his paeans to rural life were highlighted in the series "Ballads of the Byways." A fellow *News* employee noted that Herschell was a true democrat, a friend to everyone from bank presidents to truckers and a person who could "rub elbows with prominent men at some important banquet, and the next day revel in a picnic at [Indianapolis's] Douglass park." The poetry Herschell wrote for the newspaper was collected and published in a number of books during his lifetime, including *Songs of the Streets and Byways* (1915), *The Kid Has Gone to the Colors and Other Verse* (1917), *The Smile Bringer and Other Bits of Cheer* (1919), *Meet the Folks* (1924) and *Hitch and Come In* (1928). A posthumous collection, *Song of the Morning and Other Poems*, which was put together by his widow, appeared in 1940.

Known simply as Bill to his friends inside and outside the newspaper, Herschell won the esteem of readers through his simple verses, flavored as they were with the dialect style pioneered so successfully by Riley. "There was no dullness where he was and there were no dead lines in what he wrote," Brown said of Herschell, who became well known for his laugh, described by Brown as a "musical roar" that "preceded him wherever he appeared." Profiling Herschell for a biographical pamphlet produced by the *News* in 1926, B. Wallace Lewis described him as looking "more like the manager of a successful retail store than a poet. He is big, with the kind of bigness that goes clear through. A round head, hair trimmed close, joins to a massive trunk with a powerful neck. The hands that once wielded a machinist's hammer are strong and grip yours as if they meant it."

With America's entry into World War I, the subject of Herschell's writing began to turn more and more to wartime matters. He produced for the *News* such poems as "The Service Flag" and "The Kid Has Gone to the Colors." His most successful effort, however, came after he spent time at Indianapolis's Fort Benjamin Harrison, which then served as an officers' training camp. Herschell became close friends with the camp's commander, Major General Edwin F. Glenn. The two men often spent a part of each morning discussing news about the war and what was going on at the camp. During one meeting on May 18, 1917, Glenn asked Herschell to use his talents to write a war song. "These boys out here," Glenn said, "are sick of singing about 'Mother Dear' and 'Broken Hearts' and 'Gentle Eyes of Blue.' Give us something that will keep down homesickness, the curse of an army camp."

As he crossed the parade ground on his way to return to the office, Herschell spied a company of tall soldiers passing by, which gave him the inspiration to write about the army's "long boys." Driving back to downtown Indianapolis, he began to formulate the song's words and sang them to *News* photographer Paul Schideler. Charles Dennis, who worked just a few desks down from Herschell at the newspaper, remembered the day the reporter came back from Fort Harrison to work on the song "with pursed lips and corrugated brow, his blue eyes in a fine frenzy rolling." After seeing Herschell finish his writing, Dennis slipped into a chair next to the poet to view and hear the final result. "As he voiced the verses the workers in this hive of industry gathered about him," said Dennis. "Other workers from various parts of the building came in. He was obliged to sing it over and over again and though his throat became raw and raucous he

The cover to the sheet music for Herschell's song "Long Boy" featured artwork of a soldier by noted Hoosier cartoonist and illustrator Gaar Williams. *Indiana Historical Society.*

kept his good humor through seventeen recalls, and the curtain went down amid the most appreciative applause."

The next day, Herschell submitted his work, titled "Long Boy," for Glenn's review. The general took an immediate liking to the song, especially the chorus line: "I may not know what th' war's about, / But you bet, by gosh, I'll soon find out." Several members of Glenn's staff also expressed their satisfaction with the song, and the general asked Herschell to find someone to set the words to music so his troops could sing it on parade. Herschell responded by turning the lyrics over to Bradley Walker, an Indianapolis composer, who produced the music for the song. Just a week later, the troops at Fort Harrison sang "Long Boy" as they passed in review before Ohio governor James M. Cox. The song became an instant success, selling more than 1 million copies. Wabash College honored Herschell for his war verse by awarding him an honorary degree.

Herschell died on December 2, 1939, at his Indianapolis home. His last words to his wife were, "I'll whip it yet, Jo." Reminiscing about Herschell's life, the newspaper he served for so many years said that he had been a part of Indianapolis as much as the Indiana Soldiers and Sailors Monument. "He loved writing," said the *News*, "he loved to compose his sincere verse, but most of all he loved people. Otherwise he could not have written so inspiringly of their lives."

JOHN HUDDLESTON AND
THE NATIONAL ROAD

Farmer and lapsed Quaker John Huddleston was worried. Travelers that had stopped at his Wayne County, Indiana farmhouse the night before had departed at daybreak and left behind bread they had baked in the oven at the Huddleston Farm, which had become a regular stopping point for travelers on the National Road. "Hastily saddling a horse," according to Lee Burns in his history of the National Road in Indiana, "he [Huddleston] followed them with the bread only to discover that their hurried departure had been caused by the fact that they had taken his best set of harness."

Born in 1807 near Greensboro, North Carolina, John Huddleston grew up in a farming family. He was eight years old when his Quaker family migrated from North Carolina to Union County, Indiana, as part of "the great Quaker Migration," one of many such waves of migration by Quakers to eastern Indiana during the early nineteenth century. In March 1830, Huddleston married fellow Quaker Susannah Moyer in her parents' home a few miles east of Liberty, Indiana. Soon after his marriage, Huddleston was disowned by the Quaker Yearly Meeting for "disunity" with the religion's discipline. The couple lived in Union County until 1835, when Huddleston, an early Hoosier entrepreneur, decided to take advantage of a new highway just completed to Indianapolis: the National Road (today known as U.S. 40).

The idea for a roadway linking eastern manufacturers with western markets was first broached by George Washington as early as 1755. It took until 1802, however, for the idea to take shape. Congress, in the act it passed

In the 1940s, the Huddleston House on the National Road in Cambridge City, Indiana, was used to sell antiques. *Indiana Historical Society, P0411.*

creating Ohio, provided that 5 percent of the funds received by the federal government from public land sales in the state would be used to build public roads from the Atlantic Ocean to Ohio. Similar provisions were placed into the acts incorporating the states of Indiana, Illinois and Missouri. In 1803, Congress made the first appropriation for a highway across the Allegheny Mountains to Ohio—the National Road. Beginning in Cumberland, Maryland, and running through six states, the road cost about $7 million.

The National Road—also called the National Pike, Old Pike and the Cumberland Road—was an immediate hit with travelers, freight wagoners, express carriers and mail coach drivers. "The road became a busy thoroughfare," noted Burns. "Wagonhouse yards were located along the line, where the tired horses rested over night beside their great loads, and taverns, famous in their day, were built at convenient points for the stages, that were constantly arriving and departing." Not everyone, however, was pleased with the road's quality. A familiar chant about the National Road in Indiana went, "The roads are impassable / Hardly jackassable; / I think those that travel 'em / Should turn out and gravel 'em."

The National Road in Indiana traveled due west from the Ohio state line to Indianapolis, passing through such Hoosier cities as Richmond and Centerville and on to Terre Haute. Huddleston became one of many in Indiana who tried to wring a financial advantage out of the road. Along with his parents and many of his brothers' and sisters' families, he moved his young family to the town of Dublin. In 1838, Huddleston bought seventy acres along the National Road, just west of Cambridge City. His new farm included four acres with frontage along the highway.

The Huddlestons lived in a log house on their farm while a new brick house, barn and outbuildings were being erected. The 125,000 bricks used for the buildings were fired on site, and the lumber and stone used in construction were taken from the land and nearby quarries. The Huddleston farm was built to be more than a place for raising crops—it was set up to serve travelers. The barn had extra stalls for tired draft animals, the house contained two basement kitchens for rental by families and the smokehouse, outdoor oven and outhouse were all scaled to serve travelers as well as the family.

Although convenient for travelers, the Huddleston Farm's accommodations were far from plush. Families bought food to prepare in the public kitchens or paid to eat at the Huddlestons' table. In bad weather, travelers slept in the barn, on the house's porches or in its lower level. Usually they slept in their wagons parked in the barnyard. The Huddleston family's living quarters were on the house's upper two floors.

A view of the south wall of the kitchen at the Huddleston House. *Library of Congress.*

The former Quaker did well in his new home. By the time the federal agricultural census was taken in 1850, Huddleston had one of the most productive farms in the township, producing twenty tons of hay, two hundred pounds of cheese and one hundred pounds of butter. Along with his farming and lodging business, he helped support his family, which eventually numbered twelve children, by carting goods to and from Cincinnati and working on the National Road. Family histories state that Huddleston refused to carry tobacco or liquor on his trips to and from the city. They also report that his work on the road consisted of grading the long hill on Dublin's east side.

John Huddleston died in 1877 from complications resulting from an injury sustained when a family horse kicked him in the head. His wife, Susannah, died in 1892. The children divided the estate equally. After being sold out of the Huddleston family in 1934, the farm served many purposes; at various times, it was a rental property, an antiques store and a restaurant. In the 1960s, Eli Lilly, Indianapolis pharmaceutical businessman and philanthropist, became interested in helping save the Huddleston Farm. With his guidance and generous gift, Historic Landmarks Foundation, a nonprofit organization that encourages and participates in a number of statewide preservation projects, was able to buy the farm in 1966. The foundation continues to own the Huddleston Farmhouse, which is open to the public for tours.

INDIANA AND THE CIVIL WAR

The free and legal election of a Republican—Abraham Lincoln of Illinois—to the office of president in November 1860 caused many southern states to threaten to withdraw from the Union. Once free, they planned to form a nation dedicated to preserving and spreading the institution of slavery. One month after Lincoln's victory, South Carolina became the first state to secede. Other southern states soon followed. In February 1861, Jefferson Davis, a former U.S. senator, was named the new president of the Confederate States of America.

Although politicians on both sides attempted to avoid bloodshed, they could not reach agreement on a compromise. At 4:30 a.m. on April 12, 1861, Confederate forces started the American Civil War by firing on Fort Sumter, a Union military base located outside the entrance to the harbor at Charleston, South Carolina. Just two days later, after suffering severe damage from four thousand shells, Federal forces surrendered. The American flag came down, and the Confederacy's new Stars and Bars banner flew over the fort.

The attack on Fort Sumter caused those in the North to quickly rally to protect the Union. President Lincoln called for 75,000 volunteers to enlist for ninety days to meet the national emergency. Each state worked to fill its quota of soldiers called for by the president. The State of Indiana planned to fill the ranks of six regiments, about 4,600 men. "Soldiers, or good men willing to be converted into soldiers for the emergency," noted one Indiana newspaper, "seem to spring up out of the ground, eager to protect the flag and

An 1861 portrait of Indiana governor Oliver P. Morton, a devoted supporter of the Union cause during the Civil War. *Brady-Handy photograph collection, Library of Congress, Prints and Photographs Division.*

conquer the peace." Governor Oliver P. Morton, a Republican and strong supporter of the president, named Lew Wallace, a Mexican-American War veteran and son of a former governor, to serve as the state's adjutant general in charge of raising the needed number of troops.

The state fairgrounds on the near north side of the city became a camp for the new volunteers. The site became known as Camp Morton. Wallace made arrangements so that when officers and their men arrived at Indianapolis's central railroad station, they were greeted by either a brass band or a fife and drum corps. In only a short time, Indiana had raised double the number of troops called for by Lincoln. Hoosier regiments served in both the eastern and western theaters of the war and participated in such major engagements as Shiloh, Antietam, Chancellorsville, Fredericksburg, Chickamauga and Gettysburg. Many rose to top ranks in the Union army and earned distinction in battle, including Wallace, Benjamin Harrison, Jefferson C. Davis, Robert H. Milroy and Joseph J. Reynolds.

Of the nearly 300,000 men of military age in the state, 197,141 served, ranking Indiana second among Northern states in providing men for the Union cause. Another 100,000 offered their service to the state militia, defending the state from the possibility of raids by Confederate troops across the Ohio River from Kentucky. During the four years of the war, 25,025 Hoosiers died. Of that number, 7,243 died during battle, while the majority fell victim to disease.

Those who remained behind on the homefront—including wives, mothers and daughters—did what they could for the men who fought. Many women offered their services as nurses or volunteered their time with the Indiana Sanitary Commission, an organization that provided needed materials for troops preparing for battle and those who were sick or injured. Women also left their homes to work in war-related industries, especially the state arsenal established by Morton in Indianapolis to supply ammunition.

Indiana regiments played significant roles in both the eastern and western theaters of the war. In the East, the Nineteenth Indiana Volunteer Infantry Regiment became part of the famed Iron Brigade, which was made up of regiments entirely from the West. The Nineteenth suffered severe casualties to its ranks at the Battle of Antietam and at Gettysburg, with 70 percent of the Hoosier regiment becoming casualties during the first day of fighting. The largest number of Indiana troops, however, fought in western campaigns, including successful Union campaigns against Fort Henry and Fort Donelson, the Siege of Vicksburg and General William Tecumseh Sherman's march to Atlanta.

At the war's outbreak, Morton, the first native-born Hoosier to serve as the state's chief executive, called on Republicans and Democrats to abandon partisanship and join together to support the Union. Some members of the opposition responded to the governor's overture, but many Democrats were suspicious of Morton's intentions and saw his growing role as a threat to individual liberty. Democrats were also united in keeping the conflict from

Portrait of the men of Company C of the Eighty-Fourth Indiana Volunteer Infantry Regiment during the Civil War. Organized in Indianapolis, the regiment fought in such engagements as Chickamauga, Kennesaw Mountain and Peachtree Creek. *Indiana Historical Society, P0455.*

becoming a war to free the slaves. In April 1861, both the House and Senate approved a resolution stating that troops from Indiana should not be used "in any aggression upon the institution of slavery or any other constitutional right belonging to any of the states."

For his part, Morton did whatever he could—by constitutional or other means—to support the Lincoln administration and retain GOP control in Indiana. He charged that the state was infested with individuals (many Democrats) whose loyalties were to the Confederacy. Morton also hinted at the existence of such treasonable secret societies as the Knights of the Golden Circle and the Sons of Liberty. Those who opposed the governor's power and policies or offered criticism were treated as disloyal. As a means to head off any opposition, Morton suspended the writ of habeas corpus and authorized military authorities to arrest ordinary citizens.

During the 1863 session of the Indiana General Assembly, the Democrats, who controlled the legislature, sought to strip from Morton control of the state militia. To halt such an action, Republican lawmakers, hoping to prevent a quorum so legislation could pass, abandoned the capital and journeyed to Madison, Indiana. The community offered the GOP members a safe haven where they could flee across the Ohio River to Kentucky if any authorities attempted to force their return to Indianapolis.

Confederate general John Hunt Morgan and his troops terrorized southern Indiana communities in the summer of 1863. Morgan surrendered to Union forces near Salineville, Ohio, on July 26, 1863.

Without the necessary legislators to pass legislation, the session ended without the passage of any appropriation bills to fund state government. Instead of calling a special session to address the crisis, Morton relied on loans from such New York City bankers as James F.D. Lanier, formerly of Madison, and aid from the federal government to keep the state financially solvent. The legislature did not meet again for two years.

In July 1863, Morton's claims of secret societies plotting against his administration and the Union cause were put to the test when Confederate general John Hunt Morgan led two thousand cavalry troops across the Ohio River at Mauckport and into southern Indiana. Morgan's men seized supplies and looted stores in several Indiana towns, including Corydon, Salem, Vernon and Versailles. Fear spread that Morgan might turn north for Indianapolis with an aim toward releasing Confederate prisoners of war housed at Camp Morton.

Morgan's Raid, as it came to be known, failed to set off any uprising by Southern sympathizers. Instead, Hoosiers from all parts of the state rose to meet and repel the invaders. Within a few days, about sixty-five thousand men had gathered to oppose the Confederate invasion. Before the force could move against Morgan, he and his men had crossed into Ohio, where they were captured.

THE AMERICAN DIPLOMAT

JOHN HAY

D r. Charles Hay, after an arduous horse ride from his home in Lexington, Kentucky, arrived in the small town of Salem, Indiana, which at that time numbered about eight hundred inhabitants, on June 5, 1829. The young doctor managed to set up his practice shortly after his arrival on the Hoosier scene, but in the twelve years he resided in Salem, Hay barely managed to earn a living, eventually moving his practice and family to Warsaw, Illinois. Although a failure in Salem, Hay did achieve his life's ambition. "I have hoped," he wrote on his seventy-fifth birthday, "to leave behind me children, and children's children—and the greater the number, the better I would be pleased—with whom intelligence, honor, and thrift would be matters of instinct and tradition."

Born on October 12, 1838, John Hay, the third of six children raised by Charles and Helen Leonard Hay, more than met his father's wish for success. In a diplomatic/political career that spanned this country's transformation from an agrarian nation to a worldwide industrial power, John Hay worked tirelessly to see that markets remained open to burgeoning American trade—as Hay described it, to ensure "a fair field and no favor." Private secretary to Abraham Lincoln, author of the acclaimed *Pike County Ballads*, editorial writer for the *New York Tribune*, successful businessman, United States minister to Great Britain and secretary of state under two strong presidents—William McKinley and Theodore Roosevelt—Hay is best known for helping to strengthen ties between America and England, as well as his "Open Door" notes regarding trade in China.

A circa 1904 portrait of Secretary of State John Hay. He died in office in 1905. *Library of Congress.*

The diplomatic success enjoyed by this "great American gentleman" is mixed at best. While minister to Great Britain, Hay did help cement Anglo-American cooperation but failed to win several agreements desired by the United States government. Although his actions regarding China were popular with the American public, Hay's "Open Door" notes—actually written by a State Department assistant and an Englishman—did little to stop China's dismemberment by European powers. The path Hay took from a boyhood on the frontier to the pinnacle of American diplomacy is a fascinating one, however, as it offers a blueprint on how to win friends and influence people long before Dale Carnegie. "Hay never started at the bottom of anything," his biographer, Taylor Dennett, said of his subject. "He never had to."

Although his father eked out a living as a country doctor, Hay's childhood memories were bucolic ones of days passed near the banks of the Mississippi River. "The boys of my day," he recalled, "led an amphibious life in and near its [the Mississippi's] waters in the summer time, and in the winter its dazzling ice bridge, of incomparable beauty and purity, was our favorite playground." Encouraged by his father, who possessed an extensive personal library, Hay became a voracious reader and displayed an aptitude for learning foreign languages, especially Latin, Greek and German. From an early age, he also possessed the ability, as his sister observed, "of stringing words together into rhymes"—a habit he made pay in later years by writing best-selling poetry.

With his academic talents outstripping Warsaw's limited local schools, Hay, through financial assistance from his uncle Milton Hay, a prosperous Springfield, Illinois lawyer, was sent in 1849 to study at the Pittsfield Private Academy in Pike County, Illinois. The aid offered by his uncle was the first in a series of incidents in which Hay's talents would be recognized by those who could help further his career. Hay helped himself along by becoming what Elihu Root termed "the most delightful of companions," able to forge friendships that lasted a lifetime. After some college-level study at Springfield, Hay journeyed east at age seventeen to attend Brown University in Providence, Rhode Island. Hay found that life at the eastern university, he wrote to his family, "suits me exactly. The Professors are all men of the greatest ability, & what is more, perfect gentlemen."

Graduating from Brown University in 1858, Hay returned to Illinois and pondered what to do with his life. Although he considered becoming a minister or returning to the East to try his hand as a writer, his family urged him to study law instead. "They would spoil a first-class preacher," Hay wrote a friend, "to make a third-class lawyer of me." Bending to his family's wishes, Hay moved to Springfield to read law in his uncle's successful office (located adjacent to the law firm of Lincoln & Herndon).

Life back in the Midwest, however, was a far cry from what Hay had experienced while rubbing elbows with the gentlemen attending Brown. Decrying the crass materialism he believed inundated the frontier, Hay expressed to his friend Nora Perry back in Providence that by living among the barbarians in the West he would "turn from 'the rose and the rainbow' to corner-lots and tax-titles, and a few years will find my eye not rolling in a fine frenzy, but steadily fixed on the pole-star of humanity, $!" He denigrated the typical westerner as someone who "always spells badly and rides well" and possesses "profound contempt for goodness and grammar."

Despite his complaints about wasting away in Springfield, Hay was in the perfect spot in which to find a means for escaping western life. His uncle's law firm was one of the most prestigious in the state, counting as its former partners two Illinois governors and Lincoln himself. Hay used his uncle's friendship with Lincoln, and his own with John Nicolay, Lincoln's private secretary, to secure an appointment as the president's assistant private secretary. Hay had finally managed to find a way back to his beloved East.

From a seemingly innocuous position as assistant private secretary, Hay, during the trying days of the Civil War, worked his way into Lincoln's good graces, gradually handling more difficult assignments than just routine correspondence—dealing with office seekers, investigating alleged secret societies plotting against the Union cause and traveling to Canada with *New York Tribune* editor Horace Greeley to meet with Confederate representatives on a possible peace proposal. Under the president's tutelage, Hay received "a graduate course in the art of living."

Hay learned his lessons well, becoming friendly with Secretary of State William Seward—a friendship that blossomed into a job as secretary of the American legation in Paris following Lincoln's assassination. Other diplomatic posts followed in quick succession: *chargé d'affaires* at Vienna and secretary of the legation at Madrid. His experiences abroad made him an attractive catch for Greeley's *Tribune*, where Hay became an assistant editor in October 1870.

While at the *Tribune*, Hay won literary fame with such dialect poems as "Little Breeches" and "Jim Bludso." In his editorials written for the newspaper, Hay developed a politically independent reputation through his support for a wide variety of reform measures. Hay, who would later be known as the "Republican laureate" for his Lincoln biography (coauthored

President Abraham Lincoln poses with his secretaries Hay (*right*) and John Nicolay, November 1863. Hay noted in his diary that the photos taken of the president at Alexander Gardner's studio were "some of the best I have ever seen" of the president. *Library of Congress.*

by Nicolay) and relentless attacks on the Democrats, went so far as to vote for Democrat Samuel Tilden in his race for governor of New York. Hay continued to chart a politically independent course upon his move to Cleveland in the summer of 1875 with his new wife, Clara Louise Stone, daughter of Cleveland railroad tycoon Amasa Stone.

Joining his father-in-law's business, Hay became a wealthy man himself in the process. The work was far from strenuous, however, as Hay related in a letter to his friend Alvey Adee: "I am here in a nice little shop where I do nothing but read and yawn in the long intervals of work, an occupation that fits me like a glove. My work is merely the care of investments which are so safe that they require no care." With time on his hands, Hay continued to write for the *Tribune* and pursue politics.

Eventually coming to dislike life in Cleveland (Dennett described Hay as "a spiritual outlander" in that midwestern city), Hay looked for any opportunity to return to Washington, D.C. His independent political stand, however, especially his opposition to fellow Ohioan Rutherford B. Hayes, elected to the presidency in 1876, kept him out of office. When a position as American minister to Berlin opened in December 1878, Whitelaw Reid, *Tribune* publisher, suggested to Secretary of State William Evarts that Hay be given the job. Evarts refused Reid's suggestion, noting that Hay "had not been active enough in political efforts."

Stung by this rejection, Hay abandoned his political independence for that of a party regular, traveling the country giving speeches blasting the Democrats. Impressed by Hay's return to the GOP fold, Hayes in October 1879 named Hay to replace the outgoing assistant secretary of state Frederick Seward. Hay remained in that post until March 31, 1881, when President James Garfield took office.

Along with his burning desire to hold political office, Hay's return to Republican orthodoxy was also influenced by labor unrest that swept the country in 1877. "I feel that a profound misfortune and disgrace has fallen on the country, which no amount of energy or severity can now wholly remedy," Hay wrote to his father-in-law about the strikes. As he had when he returned to Illinois from college, Hay displayed his disregard for those not in his social class when he proclaimed that the "very devil seems to have entered the lower classes of working men." The strikes so unsettled Hay that he began work on a novel, *The Bread-winners: A Social Study* (published in 1883), blasting labor unions and their leaders.

Although close to Garfield, Hay was left in the political wilderness after his stint as assistant secretary of state ended in 1881. His political aspirations were hamstrung by his support for such losing presidential contenders as James Blaine and John Sherman. Hay managed to keep busy, not only producing *The Bread-winners* but also working with Nicolay on a history of Lincoln, published serially in *Century* magazine for which the duo received the then staggering sum of $50,000. Hay could afford to live a life of leisure. Upon his father-in-law's death in 1883, Hay and his wife inherited $3.5 million—money Hay would put to good use in furthering his political ambitions.

Betting his political future on Governor William McKinley of Ohio, Hay used his fortune to help ensure that the former congressman enjoyed a swift rise to the nation's top office. In 1893, McKinley found himself deeply in debt after a friend, whose note for approximately $100,000 he had endorsed, went bankrupt. Realizing that a debt-ridden McKinley would never be a successful presidential contender, his wily political handler, Mark Hanna, called on Hay and other wealthy Republicans to come to McKinley's aid.

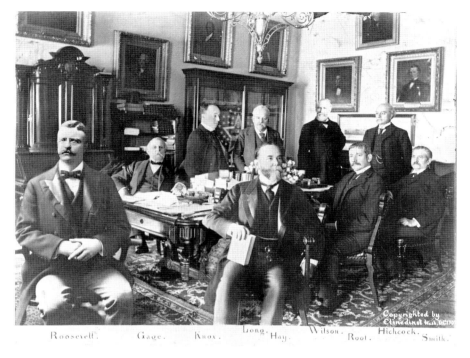

Roosevelt.   Gage.   Knox.   Long. Hay.   Wilson. Root.   Hichcock. Smith.

President Theodore Roosevelt poses with members of his cabinet, including Hay, seated to the president's right, November 1901. *Library of Congress.*

In 1897, McKinley appointed Hay as ambassador to England—an American diplomatic post then second only in importance to that of secretary of state. "I would give six-pence," Adams (a Democrat) proclaimed, "to know how much Hay paid for McKinley. His politics must have cost." Whatever the final cost, it was worth it; after only a year and a half as ambassador, Hay was called back to America to serve as McKinley's secretary of state, a post he held until his death in 1905.

Hay's time in England, at first glance, was a failure. He was unable to achieve agreements on two problems that occurred during his tenure: American claims against Canadians hunting Alaskan seals and an attempt to organize an international conference on bimetallism (the free coinage of silver). One of his few successes came during the Spanish-American War, when Britain remained neutral, and afterward, when the English government acquiesced to America's decision to hold the Philippines.

Hay's real success as an ambassador came not in reaching binding agreements with the British but in continuing to push for Anglo-American solidarity. In a speech in London in April 1898, Hay hit on that theme: "We [England and the United States] are bound by a tie which we did not forge and which we cannot break; we are joint ministers of the same sacred mission of liberty and progress, charged with duties which we cannot evade by the imposition of irresistible hands." The one "indispensable" feature of America's foreign policy, Hay wrote privately while secretary of state, "should be a friendly understanding with England"—something he achieved in his seventeen months as ambassador.

On September 30, 1898, Hay was formally sworn in as McKinley's new secretary of state, replacing William R. Day, who left to become one of the commissioners to the peace conference with Spain. The State Department of Hay's day was a small department numbering about sixty employees and unprepared for the modern age. "The typewriter was viewed as a necessary evil and the telephone was an instrument of last resort," Dennett noted. Along with inertia at the State Department, Hay had to deal with the U.S. Senate, a body he believed tried too often to interfere in the administration's conduct of foreign affairs, as well as various politicians' demands for patronage jobs. Despairing at the work facing Hay, Adams claimed that "converting an old Mississippi-raft of a confederate government into a brand-new ten-thousand-ton, triple screw, armoured, line of battleship is the work of a hundred years."

Hay brought with him to his new post, however, a philosophy that attempted to move the department into the twentieth century and further America's growing status as a world power. "We have kept always in view," the secretary of state told the New York Chamber of Commerce in 1901, "that our normal activities are in the direction of trade and commerce; that the vast development of our industries imperatively demands that we shall not only retain and confirm our hold on our present markets, but seek constantly…to extend our commercial interests in every practicable direction." Also, Hay was able to craft a staff to his liking, with such friends as William Rockhill (as a Far East expert) and Alvey Adee (as assistant secretary).

The major test of Hay's diplomatic talents during his seven years in office came on a matter pertaining to America's quest for expanded markets for its products: the carving up of China by European powers. Although the secretary of state had to deal with "the howling fools in the Senate" on such issues as aborting the 1850 Clayton-Bulwer Treaty with Britain to clear the way for an American-controlled isthmian canal, in the case of China, Hay judiciously maneuvered to keep negotiations as far removed from involvement by that legislative body as possible.

A portrait of his former boss, Lincoln, hangs on the wall behind Hay's desk in his office at the State Department. *Library of Congress.*

On March 8, 1898, shortly before the Spanish-American War broke out, the English government sent a confidential inquiry to American secretary of state John Sherman warning that certain "foreign Powers may restrict the opening of China to the commerce of all nations." The memorandum went on to ask whether the British "could count on the co-operation of the United States in opposing such action by foreign Powers and whether the United States would be prepared to join with Great Britain in opposing such measures should the contingency arise." Preoccupied with the coming war with Spain, Sherman and President McKinley declined Britain's offer, noting that they were sticking to "our traditional policy of respecting foreign alliances and so far as practicable avoiding interference or connection with European complications." Rebuffed by the Americans, the British joined the scramble for their own sphere of influence in China.

American policy in China changed, however, when Hay moved into the secretary of state's office. The successful conclusion of the war with Spain had given the United States an opportunity for a Pacific empire; McKinley, with Hay's approval, decided to take the Philippines and make "the extension of American markets in the Far East a leading policy of his administration." Although Hay, as a businessman, supported any opportunities for increasing American trade, he had little knowledge of China. For aid in formulating the McKinley administration's response to the threat posed to the open door by European powers, he turned to Rockhill, who had served as second secretary of the Peking legation in 1884.

Rockhill received help in his deliberations from Alfred E. Hippisley, a British citizen and member of the Chinese Imperial Maritime Customs Service, who visited his American friend in the summer of 1899. "I went over as frequently as I could to Washington [from his wife's family home in Baltimore]," Hippisley recalled, "to discuss the conditions in China with him [Rockhill] and especially what could be done to maintain the 'open door' or equality of opportunity for all nations in that country." Working from a memorandum on China drawn up by Hippisley, Rockhill prepared his own version for Hay, which the secretary of state distributed to Germany, Great Britain, France and Italy on September 6, 1899, and to Japan on November 17, 1899—a diplomatic notice seeking an equal economic playing field for all nations trading in China that became known as the first "Open Door" note.

The note, which had been met with popular acclaim in America, offered no serious deviation from standard American policy. Hay's true diplomatic skill on this issue came not from the writing of the note, for which credit belongs to Rockhill and Hippisley, but in his dealings with the response from the European powers. Most European governments followed the lead of Great Britain, which had declared that it would agree to follow the note's dictates if the other powers also assented. With matters up in the air, Hay acted decisively. On March 20, 1900, he issued a circular proclaiming the "final and definitive" agreement from all the countries involved. A gleeful Rockhill wrote to Hippisley that "none of the European Powers are prepared to have this question made a subject of heated debate and controversy." Hay had scored a diplomatic coup.

The secretary of state had little time to enjoy his success. In the summer of 1900 in China, there occurred an outbreak of anti-foreign violence that became known as the Boxer Rebellion. With foreign compounds in China under siege, an allied military force, including five thousand American troops from Manila, organized to relieve the embattled legations. With China in disarray, various powers—especially Russia, Germany and Japan—were poised to use the disruption as an excuse for enlarging their spheres of influence in that country.

A cartoon from the humor magazine *Puck* depicts Uncle Sam with John Bull and the emperor of Japan standing beneath a flag labeled "Open Door Policy," in a tug of war contest for "Trade Supremacy" with Russia (Nicholas II), Germany (William II) and France (Felix Faure), who are being pulled through a gate labeled "Trade Restriction." *Library of Congress.*

With his carefully crafted China policy under attack, and nearing time for McKinley's reelection campaign, Hay moved to forestall China's dismemberment. On July 3, 1900, with the president's approval, he sent a circular note (the second "Open Door" note) to the various powers stating that it was the policy of the United States to preserve China's "territorial and administrative entity, protect all rights guaranteed to friendly powers by treaty and international law, and safeguard for the world the principle of equal and impartial trade with all parts of the Chinese Empire."

At first, Hay's bold move seemed to curb the European powers' appetite for dismembering China. The American press and public hailed what the *New York Journal of Commerce* called "one of the most important diplomatic negotiations of our time." Hay realized, however, that China's integrity as a nation was held by a slim thread. "The talk about 'our preeminent moral position giving us the authority to dictate to the world,'" he told Adee, "is mere flapdoodle." The policy succeeded at first only because America had a military force in China (the troops sent to relieve the besieged legations) to check the ambitions of the foreign powers, who warily circled one another in the coming years.

Even Hay came to realize that attempting to hold together the collapsing Chinese government from total foreign domination was an impossible task. Just five months after his note proclaiming America's intention to uphold China's territorial integrity, the secretary of state instructed the American minister in Peking to try to acquire a coaling station for the American navy at Samsah Bay. The idea for the station may have been dropped, but the government seemed unwilling to live up to the claims it had made in Hay's second "Open Door" note. Asked by Japan if the United States would join it in stopping Russian activity in Manchuria, Hay declined, saying that the United States was not "prepared to attempt singly, or in concert with other Powers, to enforce these views in the east by any demonstration which could present a character of hostility to any other Power." The open door Hay had touted was closing fast.

Hay's "Open Door" adventure had a far-reaching effect on American diplomacy in the Far East in the twentieth century. Instead of Hay's policy ensuring the territorial integrity of China as a failure, subsequent State Department officials made the mistake of trying to live up to a discredited policy. "The idea of preserving Chinese territorial and administrative entity, in itself a somewhat ambitious policy," noted Robert Ferrell of Indiana University, "gave way almost unconsciously to the idea of downright guarantee of Chinese territory." This policy put the United States on a collision course with another growing power in the Far East: Japan. In its own way, Hay's work started America on the path to World War II.

THE PEOPLE'S CHOICE

CONGRESSMAN JIM JONTZ

On the eve of Election Day in November 1974, Kathy Altman, volunteer White County coordinator for Democratic candidate Floyd Fithian's successful run to represent the Second Congressional District against incumbent Republican congressman Earl Landgrebe, was driving back with her husband, Jerry, to their house in Monticello, Indiana. The couple had just finished a long day's work setting up a get-out-to-vote effort on Fithian's behalf. Suddenly, the car's headlights flashed into the rainy darkness and lit upon a lonely figure trudging down the road: Jim Jontz, a young, first-time candidate for the Indiana House of Representatives.

Jontz had been staying at the Altmans' home while engaging in a dogged door-to-door campaign in the four counties of the Twentieth District. Altman and her husband asked him if he needed any help. "No, it's late," Altman remembered Jontz responding, "but there's a laundromat up there that's still open I think I'll go hit before I quit for the night."

The next day, Jontz, a twenty-two-year-old Indiana University graduate with an unpaid job as a caretaker for a local nature preserve, defeated his heavily favored Republican opponent, John M. "Jack" Guy, Indiana House majority leader. "I must have knocked on half the doors in the district," Jontz said of what he called a "shoe-leather" campaign. "And I found that people like to have someone come to their door and talk to them, even if it is a young kid. I told them that I wasn't a lawyer or politician, but that I was interested in people, in dealing with them personally. And that was about it."

Jontz had entered the race in the majority Republican district in large part to oppose a multimillion-dollar U.S. Army Corps of Engineers dam project on Big Pine Creek near Williamsport, Indiana. He had gone to bed on election night believing he had lost after hearing a report from the final precinct in Warren County indicating that he had been defeated by a scant two votes. The next morning, he awoke to learn that there had been an error—he had won by the same slim margin. "One more vote than I needed to win!" he later exclaimed. The unexpected result stunned election officials, with one deputy clerk in Warren County marveling, "I never before realized just how important that one vote can be."

As a liberal Democrat (Jontz preferred the term progressive) usually running in conservative districts, Jontz had political pundits predicting his defeat in every election only to see him celebrating another victory with his happy supporters, always clad in a scruffy plaid jacket with a hood from high school that he wore for good luck. "I always hope for the best and fight for the worst," said Jontz. He won five terms as state representative for the Twentieth District (Benton, Newton, Warren and White Counties), served two years in the Indiana Senate and captured three terms in the U.S. Congress representing the sprawling Fifth Congressional District in northwestern Indiana that stretched from Lake County in the north to Grant County in the south.

Jontz managed to win reelection in the Republican district thanks to a combination of tireless campaigning; a relentless focus on serving his constituents through such activities as town hall meetings, a toll-free number for those wishing to question their congressman and face-to-face encounters at neighborhood coffee shops at all hours of the day; and a willingness to listen to dissenting opinions. "You have to disagree sometimes," he noted. "But you have to disagree agreeably."

Tom Sugar, a longtime Jontz aide, called the congressman "very, very politically savvy, not in a sense that he manipulated voters, I don't mean that. What I mean is, he knew the people he cared about and learned their issues very deeply. And he sincerely fought for their interests. And he fought for the interests of his district." Tom Buis, an agricultural policy expert on the congressman's staff, remembered returning late at night to the Longworth House Office Building in Washington, D.C., only to find Jontz still at his desk reading every letter that went into and out of his office. "If his constituents were paying him by the hour, he was working for less than minimum wage," said Buis, "because he worked around the clock. They got their money's worth."

In every election, Congressman Jim Jontz said he tried to run on the same theme—"getting government back on the side of the average citizen." *Calumet Regional Archives, Indiana University Northwest.*

Each election season, voters in Jontz's Congressional district could count on hearing a knock on their front door and seeing the rumpled, tousle-haired Democrat ready to promote his candidacy and talk about whatever issue that might concern them that year. "Jim believed in knocking on every door that was knockable," said Sugar, who went on to serve as chief of staff for U.S. Senator Evan Bayh. Whenever a community in his district hosted a parade, Jontz could be found riding the route on his sister's rusty old blue Schwinn bicycle with mismatched tires, waving to the crowd lining the streets, his tie flapping in the breeze—an effort that won him the title of "best congressman on two wheels" from one Indiana reporter. (Jontz's record was riding his bicycle in seven Fourth of July parades in one day.)

From an early age, Jontz, the eldest of two children born to Leland, an Indianapolis businessman, and Pauline (Polly) Jontz, displayed a penchant for organization and a dedication to nature while growing up in the 1960s in the Northern Hills subdivision on the city's north side—a "semirural setting" that enabled him to develop his interest in the outdoors. "Mom encouraged me to chase butterflies, and we bought all the Golden [Nature] guidebooks," Jontz said. Polly, who worked at the Children's Museum of Indianapolis and for many years as president of the Conner Prairie Pioneer Settlement, remembered her son as "a very intense child, very curious, very serious, [and] very focused." Jontz's kindergarten teacher told his mother that he had been the only student she had taught "who had the dignity to be president of the United States." He also displayed the leadership qualities that served him well during his political career, organizing the neighborhood children for impromptu football games and bicycle races.

From his parents, Jontz learned the lesson of always following his convictions but expressing disagreement within established structures. Both Polly and Leland Jontz were staunch Republicans and were surprised to hear their son note, after saying something to him about their political party, "Mom, I'm a Democrat." Despite their political differences, his parents supported Jontz's quest to find a suitable vocation for his devotion to hard work and wide knowledge. After graduating from North Central High School, Jontz entered Williams College, a small liberal arts institution in Massachusetts, but spent only one semester there, calling it "too academic" for his tastes. "I read 12 hours a day there," Jontz recalled of his time at Williams. "I had had enough of that, so when I came to I.U. [Indiana University] I had some spare time."

In January 1971, Jontz enrolled at IU in Bloomington, where he majored in geology and lived in Wright Quad with a freshman named Bob Rodenkirk. A native of Chicago, Illinois, Rodenkirk originally had been roommates with a relative of Philippine dictator Ferdinand Marcos who very quickly flunked out of the university after spending more time enjoying himself than studying. Jontz proved to be quite different, with Rodenkirk describing him as a serious and driven student, especially when it came to environmental issues. "I can't remember a time when he didn't have a to-do list a half a mile long," said Rodenkirk, who has worked for many years as a broadcaster in his hometown.

As more and more Americans became concerned with conserving the country's natural resources, Jontz responded by spending a large amount of his time with the Biology Crisis Center, a student group working on conservation and environmental affairs in the Bloomington area. With the center he worked on such issues as the belching black smoke from the university's coal-fired power plant, a sinkhole that had emerged in front of Wright Quad, how IU disposed of plastic foodware, the ecology of the Jordan River and opposing a dam that threatened the Lost River in Orange County.

Graduating from IU in 1973 with Phi Beta Kappa honors, Jontz worked for a few months in Chicago as program director for the Lake Michigan Federation before returning to his home state as conservation director for the Indiana Conservation Council, where he also edited the organization's monthly newsletter. A potential ecological threat in Warren County, however, soon drew Jontz to northwestern Indiana. As far back as the 1930s, there had been proposals to build a dam and reservoir on Big Pine Creek, which flowed from southwestern White County south through Benton and Warren Counties before entering the Wabash River near Attica, Indiana. Along its route, the creek flowed along scenic sandstone cliffs and Fall Creek Gorge, noteworthy for the large potholes carved into the floor of the steep-sided canyon. In October 1965, Congress, in its Flood Control Act, authorized the Army Corps of Engineers to build an earth and rockfill dam on Big Pine Creek at an estimated cost of $28 million. The resulting reservoir would cover more than one thousand acres northeast of Williamsport, Indiana.

The project, which received support from Republican congressman John T. Myers representing the Seventh Congressional District, drew protests from state environmental groups and a number of citizens in Warren County (a mail poll taken by a local newspaper has residents against the dam by a ten-to-one margin). Local groups opposing the project, including the Committee on Big Pine Creek and the Friends of the Big Pine Creek, charged that the dam and its reservoir would engulf sixty homes, ten commercial properties, 2,347 acres of cropland, 2,200 acres of pastureland and 1,995 acres of woodlands. Hoping to protect a portion of the area from destruction, the Nature Conservancy, with the help of a $20,000 loan from a Purdue University janitor, bought a forty-three-acre site in Warren County, property that included Fall Creek Gorge. The conservancy hired Jontz to serve as caretaker and program director for the property.

Often dressed in his trademark blue-jean overalls, Jontz quickly became one of the leaders in the fight against the Big Pine Creek dam, dominating a Corps of Engineers hearing on the project and appearing in the forefront of a protest held during a fundraising golf event for Congressman Myers that saw dam opponents cruise around the country club in a mile-long caravan of cars, pickup trucks, motorcycles and farm implements. Protestors confronted Myers with signs reading "Only You Can Prevent Forest Floods" and "Dam the Corps."

To help give voice to those opposing the dam (a project the federal government finally abandoned), Jontz attempted to find someone to run for the state legislature against incumbent Guy, a Monticello attorney, in the rural district. Unable to secure a candidate for the Democratic nomination, he approached party leaders in the area and told them he wanted to run. "They were tickled to death that someone wanted to do it," Jontz said. With help from his wife and a few friends, Jontz began a shoe leather, door-to-door campaign, visiting every house in such small communities in the district as Boswell, Brook, Brookston, Chalmers, Fowler, Goodland, Kentland, Monon, Morocco, Otterbein, Oxford, Otterbein, Reynolds, West Lebanon, Wolcott and many others. He also attended every fish fry he could find and three straight weeks of county fairs, shaking hands with countless potential voters. "I campaigned on the personal attention idea," Jontz said. "Issues are important to people, but more important to them is feeling that government is responsive."

After his razor-thin win over Guy in the general election, Jontz worked as hard during his days as a legislator as he had during the campaign. When the legislature was not in session, he could be found back in the district, attending meetings of service clubs and any other local event he could find. Jontz often talked with voters and turned their concerns about issues into legislation. After speaking with a grade school teacher in Wolcott, Jontz introduced a bill requiring reading and writing tests for high school graduates, an idea that became law.

In 1986, GOP congressman Elwood "Bud" Hillis, who had represented the Fifth Congressional District since 1971, announced he would not seek reelection. Jontz captured the Democratic nomination for the position and faced fellow state senator James Butcher of Kokomo. Sugar, a Howard County native whose parents supported Butcher and even held a fundraiser for him in their home, recalled receiving a call from Alan Maxwell, his political science professor at IU Kokomo, saying there was a candidate running for Congress who needed his help in organizing the county. His first meeting with Jontz occurred at the Howard County 4-H Fairgrounds. "I'd seen a photo of Jim in the paper before and, bless his heart, he wasn't the most telegenic guy in the world," said Sugar, who had never before participated in a political campaign. Impressed by the candidate's passion for issues, he agreed to help with his door-to-door efforts in the county, assisted by local members of the United Auto Workers and environmentalists from Indianapolis.

On a typical day, Jontz started knocking on doors on one side of the street beginning at three o'clock in the afternoon, with Sugar or another campaign aide taking the other side. The usual spiel included introducing themselves, telling a homeowner that Jontz was campaigning in the area and giving them material on his candidacy. If someone did not answer, Jontz would leave behind his literature with a note signed, "Sorry I missed you, Jim." Sugar said that the rule of thumb was that the campaign did not "stop knocking on doors until people started showing up [dressed] in robes." After completing their first canvass of the county, every house that could be visited, Sugar quoted Jontz as indicating, "'OK, let's do it again.' So we did it again." Two days before the election, the second canvass had been completed, but Jontz decided to do it again. "He believed in working until the last dog died," said Sugar.

A typical day for Jontz when he was back in the Fifth District involved a lot of time traveling from one community to another via automobile. *Calumet Regional Archives, Indiana University Northwest.*

Just hours after the polls closed on November 4, 1986, with Jontz defeating Butcher 80,722 (51.4 percent) to 75,507 (48.1 percent), the new congressman found Sugar as the celebration at campaign headquarters in Monticello was winding down and told him he wanted to visit a Chrysler plant in Kokomo the next day to thank the workers for their support. Bright and early the next morning, after only a few hours of sleep, Jontz stood at the plant's gate to greet the groggy automotive workers as they started their early shift, jolting them awake with his words: "Hey, thanks a lot guys, I won't let you down. I really appreciate your support yesterday, I will not forget." Most of the workers acted as if this was the first time a candidate had ever thanked them personally for their vote just hours after winning an election. "It was an example of everything our campaign stood for," said Sugar. "We meant it. We're really going to fight for working folks."

While in Congress, Jontz, who twice won reelection, worked to make his mark on legislation in a similar manner as he had while serving in the Indiana legislature—through amendments, a procedure he used effectively on the 1990 Farm Bill. While other congressmen went home for the evening, Jontz stayed late until the night, even making popcorn for hungry staffers from other Congressional offices as they worked to settle differences between House and Senate versions of legislation. The staff members were not only "just floored" that they got a snack, Buis noted, but they were also astonished that "it was delivered and popped by a member of Congress. But Jim never thought of himself as someone with a title above anyone else. That was part of his appeal to people." Klose noted that Jontz also made his mark in Congress by working within the system to earn financial assistance for such projects back in his district as the Hoosier Heartland Corridor road project, the psychological unit at the veterans hospital in Marion and Grissom Air Force Base near Peru.

Although Jontz attempted to find common ground with Republican legislators, particularly on agricultural issues with GOP senator Richard Lugar, he was not afraid to vote his conscience rather than what might be popular back in his district, including voting against the use of force in the Gulf War. Jontz's firm support of environmental issues frustrated and sometimes enraged colleagues from across the aisle. His sponsorship of the Ancient Forest Protection Act, which would have forbidden cutting stands of ancient timber in three western states, caused one Oregon congressman to call him "a rank opportunist," while another member of the Oregon delegation kicked him out of his office in the middle of a heated argument. Angered by Jontz's successful push to end arrangements benefiting timber companies in the Tongass National Forest in Alaska, Congressman Don Young of that state introduced a bill to establish 35 percent of Jontz's district as a national forest. To answer charges that he was meddling in matters outside of the district he represented, Jontz called the ancient forests "a national treasure, much as the Grand Canyon, Yosemite, and the Everglades are. If we cut the last 10 percent of the ancient forests for short-term greed, they will be gone forever. If we preserve them, future generations, as well as our own, will be able to enjoy their benefits."

Jontz's life on the razor edge of politics came to an end in the 1992 election, when he was defeated by Republican challenger Steve Buyer. Several issues hurt Jontz during that campaign, including an antipolitician mood in the electorate inspired by the independent presidential candidacy of businessman Ross Perot, opposition from western carpenters unions for Jontz's stand on old-growth forests, opposition from the pharmaceutical industry after he held a town meeting to discuss the high cost of prescription drugs and a scandal involving the House bank involving a small number of overdrafts of checks. "It was the death of a thousand cuts," noted Sugar.

Jontz greets members of the Future Farmers of America at his office in Washington, D.C. A poster for the movie *Hoosiers* can be seen in the background. *Calumet Regional Archives, Indiana University Northwest.*

Reflecting on the first defeat ever in his political career, Jontz noted that he had been "skating on thin" ice for a long time as a Democrat in mainly Republican districts.

After his defeat, Jontz eventually left Indiana to battle on behalf of numerous progressive causes to forge coalitions among labor and environmental groups. He led an unsuccessful campaign to stop the passage of the North American Free Trade Agreement with the Citizens Trade Campaign, served as president of the Americans for Democratic Action and worked as executive director for the Western Ancient Forest Campaign. He participated in acts of civil disobedience, including blocking a logging road in Oregon's Siskiyou National Forest in the spring of 1995. His parents were aghast that he was arrested during the protest. Jontz tried to mollify them by noting, "I had my suit on!"

Jontz moved to Portland, Oregon, in 1999, but Indiana still had a hold on him. He told his mother that he sometimes thought of returning to the Hoosier State to buy a plot of land in the Brown County hills, where he

In 1990, Jontz participates in Earth Day activities atop Mount Baldy at the Indiana Dunes National Lakeshore. *Calumet Regional Archives, Indiana University Northwest.*

could sit back, relax and enjoy the trees. He never had that chance, dying at his home in Portland on April 14, 2007, after a two-year battle with colon cancer that had spread to his liver.

Visiting him during the former congressman's final illness, Sugar recalled walking into a Portland hospital room to see Jontz on a conference call with fellow workers in the environmental cause, offering them his ideas on what to do next. For Scott Campbell, who had served as the congressman's press secretary, hearing about Jontz's death reminded him of a campaign stop the two of them had made to one house in a small town in the Fifth District. "I've never had a congressman come to my door in the twenty-nine years that I've been an adult," Campbell remembered the homeowner telling Jontz. "When you live in some very small town like Royal Center, Indiana, and not just you, but half the town says my congressman knocked on my door today, that means something."

SWAMPED

MARQUIS DE LAFAYETTE ON THE OHIO RIVER

T he sidewheel steamboat SS *Mechanic* was a familiar sight on the Ohio River in the 1820s. On Sunday, May 8, 1825, the shallow-draft craft used its best asset—its speed—to quickly transport a French aristocrat and his traveling companions to a celebration in Louisville, Kentucky. The boat never reached its destination. Around midnight, about 125 miles from Louisville near the present-day Indiana town of Cannelton, the ship struck a submerged log and started taking on water. Although the *Mechanic*'s crew and passengers all managed to make their way safely to shore, Captain Wyllys Hall was distraught. The next morning, Hall stayed behind, sadly telling Auguste Levasseur, a French nobleman's private secretary, "Never will my fellow citizens pardon me for the peril to which Lafayette was exposed last night."

The foreign visitor who came close to losing his life on that pitch-dark, rainy night was the Marquis de Lafayette. Hero of the American and French Revolutions, the sixty-seven-year-old Lafayette had been visiting southern and western states at the time of the shipwreck as part of his triumphal grand tour of the United States. Cities (including Lafayette, Indiana), towns, villages, counties and streets were named in his honor, and communities throughout the nation competed for the pleasure of Lafayette's company at extravagant parties. Just four days after his near disaster on the Ohio River, Lafayette stopped in Jeffersonville, Indiana, for a reception that Governor James B. Ray said would be "marked by posterity, as the brightest epoch in the calendar of Indiana."

A portrait of the Marquis de Lafayette painted by Samuel F.B. Morse, inventor of the telegraph. *George Grantham Bain Collection, Library of Congress.*

For Lafayette, harassed in France by government agents and nearly penniless, the invitation to visit the country he had once fought for in its struggle for liberty was an opportunity too good to pass up. In his letter of invitation, President James Madison informed the Marquis that Congress had "passed a resolution on this subject, in which the sincere attachment of the whole nation to you is expressed, whose ardent desire is once more to see you amongst them." Lafayette and his small party, which included his son, George Washington Lafayette; his secretary, Levasseur; and his valet, Bastien, left France on July 13, 1824, aboard the *Cadmus*, an American merchant ship. After a smooth voyage, Lafayette arrived in New York on August 14.

Lafayette received an enthusiastic greeting as a "Hero of Two Worlds" for his fight on behalf of republican government in the United States and France. The old soldier also discovered early on during his more than year-long visit that he would not have to worry about expenses. On December 22, a grateful Congress passed a bill giving Lafayette $200,000 and a large tract of land in what is now Tallahassee, Florida (he later sold the property for $100,000).

After visiting New York and Washington, D.C., Lafayette left to tour the rest of the country, meeting such illustrious Americans as Andrew Jackson, whom he visited in Nashville, Tennessee, at his home, the Hermitage. On May 8, after attending a dinner in Shawneetown, Illinois, Lafayette and his traveling party boarded the *Mechanic* for the trip to Louisville. At about 10:00 p.m., according to Levasseur, George Lafayette came below after being up on deck and remarked to his father's secretary that he was surprised "that in so dark a night, our captain did not come to, or at least abate the speed of the vessel." Accustomed by now, however, to traveling in all kinds of adverse conditions, the two men turned their conversation to other matters.

Shortly after midnight, the ship's passengers were jolted awake "by a horrible shock" that stopped the vessel dead in the water on the Kentucky side of the river about fifty yards from shore. Running up on deck to learn why the boat had stopped, Levasseur was greeted by cries from fellow passengers that they had run aground on a sandbar. Seizing a light, Levasseur, joined by the captain, opened the hold and found that the ship had "half filled with water, which rushed in torrents through a large opening. 'A snag! A snag!' cried the captain, 'Hasten Lafayette to my boat! Bring Lafayette to my boat!'"

Returning to his cabin, Levasseur found Lafayette awake and beginning to be dressed by his valet. "What news?" Lafayette asked his secretary. "That we shall go to the bottom, gentlemen, if we cannot extricate ourselves, and we have not a moment to spare," Levasseur quickly responded. Lafayette, however, remained unruffled by the danger. Upon leaving his cabin, he halted on the stairs when he remembered that he had left behind on his table a snuffbox ornamented with George Washington's portrait. Levasseur and George Lafayette managed to convince the Marquis to proceed while Levasseur went back and retrieved the item.

According to Perry County legend, Lafayette, as he eased into a small lifeboat, slipped, fell into the river and nearly drowned. But Levasseur painted an entirely different picture in his account. Noting that the dark night and the small boat's instability made it difficult to step off the already listing steamboat, the secretary reported that he got into the craft, and "while the captain was keeping it as near the vessel as possible, two persons helped him [Lafayette] in, holding him by the shoulders, while I received him in my arms." As soon as Lafayette found a safe seat, the yawl pushed off from the sinking *Mechanic* and steered its way to the Indiana shore, reaching land in less than three minutes.

Lafayette, who had remained calm throughout the disaster, lost his coolness when he discovered that his son was not among the nine people on

LANDING OF GEN. LAFAYETTE,
At Castle Garden, New York, 16th August 1824.

THIS PLATE MADE FOR
THE SOCIETY OF HOOSIERS
NEW YORK 1899

An engraving of Lafayette wearing his uniform and showing a view of the scene of his arrival in New York City in 1824. *Library of Congress.*

the lifeboat. "He was filled with anxiety," Levasseur said of Lafayette, "and in a state of the most violent agitation. He began to call, 'George! George!' with all his strength." On a second trip back to the *Mechanic*, which had a small portion of its roof and wheelhouse sticking out of the water, Levasseur discovered George Lafayette calmly waiting to be rescued.

The nearly fifty crew and passengers all managed to make their way to safety, either by being rescued by the lifeboat or by swimming to shore. The survivors lit fires to dry themselves and even found a mattress, dry on one side, on which Lafayette slept. At daybreak, the passengers searched through the wreckage that covered the shoreline for their belongings, some "mournfully recounted the extent of their losses, others could not avoid laughing at the nakedness of costume in which they found themselves; this gaiety soon became prevalent…and at last smoothed the visages of the most sorrowful, and almost transformed our shipwreck into a party of pleasure," noted Levasseur.

Lafayette's unexpected appearance on Hoosier soil helped to inspire years of storytelling in Ohio River communities. After the shipwreck, according to a 1916 Perry County history, "only the simple log cabin of a sturdy pioneer, James Cavender, offered shelter to the highborn nobleman who had slept under the palace-roof of Versailles, yet Hoosier hospitality gave of its best." Also, the history claimed that the next morning, news of Lafayette's unexpected visit had spread like wildfire through the region, bringing several farmers and their children to the scene to catch a glimpse of the hero. Lafayette supposedly received his "rustic visitors" in a cleft between two rocks where a spring flowed—a site known today as Lafayette Spring.

Legend has it that Lafayette also made stops in the Indiana communities of Madison, Lawrenceburg and Vevay. Charles N. Thompson, trying to unravel the mystery in a 1928 issue of the *Indiana Magazine of History*, concluded that the Frenchman "never visited any other part of the state of Indiana than the place in the woods where he involuntarily spent the night on the shore of the Ohio River near the present site of Cannelton, and later, Jeffersonville." Thompson also cast doubt on Lafayette's stay overnight in the Cavender cabin and subsequent entertainment of local visitors.

Evidence may be speculative for Lafayette's other purported visits to Indiana communities, but it is clear that the young state pulled out all the stops in its reception for the Revolutionary War hero in Jeffersonville on May 12. Lafayette's visit was not a spur-of-the-moment affair. On January 29, 1825, Indiana governor William Henricks wrote to Lafayette informing him that the state legislature had passed a joint resolution inviting him to visit the nineteenth state. The resolution, transmitted to Lafayette by Hendricks in his letter to the general, exhibited the lawmakers' pride in their state. The legislators noted that on his trip west of the Allegheny Mountains, Lafayette would "behold extensive communities of freemen which, within the period of his own recollection, have been substituted for the trackless wilderness. Where forty years ago primeval barbarism held undisputed sway over man and nature, civilization, liberty and law wield the mild scepter of equal rights; it is here, that our illustrious friend will find his name, his services, and, we trust, his principles flourishing in perennial verdure."

The young state of Indiana provided Lafayette quite an elaborate welcome on May 12 when he visited Jeffersonville. At 11:00 a.m., Lafayette stepped off the steamboat *General Pike* and received a twenty-four-gun salute, shot three times, noted a dispatch by a Hoosier printed in the *Louisville Public Advertiser*. Under escort from three artillery companies, Lafayette journeyed to the home of the late governor Thomas Posey, located on the west corner of Front and Fort Streets overlooking the river.

Upon reaching the Posey mansion, Lafayette received formal greetings from acting Indiana governor James B. Ray, who had been thrust into the job following Hendricks's election to the U.S. Senate. After a welcoming speech by Ray and remarks from Lafayette, the general attended a reception where he met a few local citizens, including some Revolutionary War veterans.

At 3:00 p.m., Lafayette attended a dinner in the woods just above Posey's home. Following dinner, a number of toasts were made, including those to the memory of Washington, the Continental Congress, the Congress of 1824, the president of the United States and "Major General Lafayette, united with Washington in our hearts—We hail his affectionate visit with a heart-cheering welcome." Lafayette offered his own toast: "Jeffersonville and Indiana—May the rapid progress of this young state, a wonder among wonders, more and more evince the blessings of republican freedom!"

Three hours after the dinner started, Lafayette left the table and was taken back to the *General Pike* for the return trip to Louisville, where he was to be the guest of honor at a ball that evening. "Never again did Lafayette set his foot on the soil of Indiana and never again has Indiana entertained a more noble or a more distinguished guest," Thompson concluded.

RING LARDNER, SOUTH BEND
AND BASEBALL

In the spring of 1901, the University of Notre Dame varsity baseball team was busy preparing for a game on the South Bend, Indiana campus. Ed Reulbach, the team's starting pitcher and future star of the Chicago Cubs, noticed a tall, lanky youngster approach trainer Tom Holland and ask if he could have the job of water carrier. Informed that the job had already been filled, the kid sat in the grandstand for the entire game "with his overalls and farmer's sun bonnet on," Reulbach recalled.

The next day, Reulbach traveled to Niles, Michigan, a few miles north of South Bend, to pitch for the town's baseball team. Sitting on the bench before the game, somebody offered him a tin cup full of water. "I glanced at the individual and almost fell off the bench—there was the same kid I saw at the Saturday game when he asked to be a water boy," said Reulbach. "He sat next to me on the bench and offered me a cup of water every few minutes, until I finally told him that I did not need a bath, just a cup of water every other inning."

Seven years later, as a pitcher for the Cubs, Reulbach again met up with the eager water boy. He had just sat down to a poker game on a train leaving Chicago—a game that also included the famed Cubs double-play combination of Joe Tinker, Johnny Evers and Frank Chance—when he heard someone say to Tinker, "I will get you a glass of water." According to Reulbach, the voice haunted him, and he "looked up, lo and behold, there was the same water boy from Niles and Notre Dame. He smiled and said, 'Do you remember me?' I said 'Yes—but I do not need a bath.'"

During his heyday pitching for the Chicago Cubs, Ed Reulbach won twenty-four games in 1908, when the team captured the World Series—the last time it would do so until 2016. *Library of Congress.*

Reulbach had met the new baseball reporter for the *Chicago Examiner*, Ring Lardner.

Known for creating such indelible baseball characters as Jack Keefe (*You Know Me Al*), Alibi Ike and others, Lardner received his early indoctrination to the intricacies of the game by covering the Central League, a Class B minor league for the *South Bend Times*. The league—which produced such future major-league stars as Goat Anderson, Own J. "Ownie" Bush, Slow Joe Doyle, Jack Hendricks, Dan Howley and John Ganzel—provided Lardner with a training ground for learning more on how to be a reporter and how to cover a sport he had loved since childhood. "Altogether," Lardner later confided to a fellow newspaperman, "I had a lovely time on that paper."

Ringgold (later shortened to Ring) Wilmer Lardner was born on March 6, 1885, in Niles, Michigan, the youngest of nine children raised by Henry and Lena Phillips Lardner. A successful businessman, Henry provided his children with all the comforts money could buy. The family's spacious Broad Street home was located just a stone's throw from the St. Joseph River, and each child had his or her own nursemaid. From an early age, Ring and his brother Rex developed a mania for baseball. Ring claimed that even when he and his brother were being pushed around Niles in baby carriages, the two "could rattle off the batting order of any of the National Leagues' twelve clubs."

Although born with a deformed foot and forced to wear a brace until he was eleven years old, Ring did take part in such activities as baseball and swimming. As the children of privilege, however, the three youngest Lardners were not allowed to, as Ring put it, "mingle with the tough eggs from the West Side and Dickereel [a poorer German neighborhood in Niles]." The Lardner children's insulation from the harsh life outside their home extended to their education. Instead of attending local primary schools, Ring, Rex and their sister Anna were taught by a private tutor named Harry Mansfield. Nicknamed "Beady" by his young charges, the tutor came to the house "every morning at 9 and stayed till noon and on acct. of it taking him 2 and a 1/2 hrs. to get us to stop giggling," Lardner remembered.

The private lessons offered by Mansfield did not seem to help when the Lardners took their examinations to enter high school—they all flunked. A kindhearted principal, however, relented and placed Ring and Anna in the ninth grade and Rex in the tenth grade on a probationary basis. Despite their sheltered early life, Ring and his siblings flourished in their new surroundings. In addition to playing on the football team, Ring, Rex, Ed Wurz and Ray Starkweather formed a quartet that spent many nights

Ring Lardner at age twenty-eight during his days as the writer of the column "In the Wake of the News" for the *Chicago Tribune. Everett Collection Historical/Alamy Stock Photo.*

serenading Niles's young female population. Hardly an evening passed, said Lardner, when "some gal's father did not feel himself called on to poke his head out his Fourth Street window and tell these same boys to shut up and go home for the sake of a leading character in the Bible."

If Lardner became tired of his hometown's late-night offerings, he could always hitch up a horse and buggy and set off for South Bend's bright lights. Convincing the family's horse, Fred, to trot at a pace suitable to see a date home before curfew, however, proved to be a difficult task. On one occasion, Lardner did not get his date home until 3:30 a.m., "which was at that time," he noted, "the latest which either she or I or Fred had been up, but mother was still sitting up and I tried to tell her the old proverb how you can trot a horse to South Bend but you can't trot him home but she couldn't hear me on acct. of somebody talking all the time." It was the last time Lardner dated that girl.

After graduation, Lardner turned down a scholarship offer from Olivet College. Times were hard for the Lardner family. Henry's eldest son, William, a Duluth, Minnesota banker, had convinced his father to invest heavily in the institution. The bank's failure, coupled with a bad investment in a Canadian mining operation, forced Henry to sell his large landholdings to pay off his creditors. Ring's early attempts to make a living did not help matters. He worked in Chicago as an office boy for the McCormick Harvester Company and the Peabody, Houghteling and Company real estate firm, but he was fired after only a few weeks. Returning to Niles, he found a job with the Michigan Central Railroad at a salary of one dollar per day. The railroad fired him, however, for, as he described it, "putting a box of cheese in the through Jackson car, when common sense should have told me that it ought to go to Battle Creek."

In January 1902, Lardner's father scraped together enough money to send both Ring and Rex to the Armour Institute in Chicago to study engineering, an occupation for which both proved to be ill-suited. "I can't think of no walk in life for which I had more of a natural bent unless it would be hostess at a roller rink," Ring observed. Instead of hitting the books, the brothers spent most of their time in Chicago taverns and theaters. By the spring, the two had flunked out of the institute and returned to Niles.

Although Rex was able to find a job as a reporter for the *Niles Daily Sun*, as well as being the Niles correspondent for the *Kalamazoo Gazette* and the *South Bend Tribune*, Ring spent the next year recovering "from the strain which had wrought havoc with my nervous system." He found time to write and perform with a local musical group called the American Minstrels, which organized performances at the Niles Opera House. In 1904, he took a job with the Niles Gas Company at five dollars a week, later raised to eight dollars a week. The only trouble Lardner had with his job came in reading meters, usually located in "dark cellars where my favorite animal, the rat, is wont to dwell. When I entered a cellar and saw a rat reading the meter ahead of me, I accepted his reading and went on to the next house."

Lardner might have spent the remainder of his life avoiding rats in dark basements were it not for a happy accident involving his reporter brother, Rex. In the fall of 1905, Edgar Stoll, son of *South Bend Times* owner John B. Stoll, visited Niles to try to convince Rex to quit his job and work for the *Times*. Rex was on vacation at the time, so the *Niles Daily Sun* editor sent Edgar Stoll to visit Ring at the gas company for more information. Ring's newspaper career came out of this one chance meeting. He remembered:

> *Mr. Stoll sought me out and stated his errand, also inquiring whether my brother was tied up to a contract* [with the *Daily Sun*]. *I said yes, which*

*was the truth. I asked how much salary he was willing to offer. He said
twelve dollars a week. Why?*

"Oh," I said, "I thought I might tackle the job myself."

"Have you ever done any newspaper work?"

*"Yes, indeed," I said. "I often help my brother." This was very far from
the truth, but I was thinking of those rats.*

Lardner, who obtained the job at a salary of $12 a week, seemed
undisturbed about his venture into a new career. "I had no newspaper
experience, but a two years' course in a gas-office teaches you practically
all there is to know about human nature," he noted. "Besides, I had been
class poet at the high school, and I knew I could write." Lardner's family
had other worries. Although agreeing that $12 a week was $4 more than
what he was earning at the gas company, they pointed out that traveling to
work on the interurban railroad linking Niles and South Bend cost $2.40
per week, and instead of eating free at home, he would have to pay for his
lunches. Lardner, having given his word to Edgar Stoll, brushed aside these
financial concerns and accepted the job on the *Times* as a self-described
"sporting editor and staff, dramatic critic, society and court-house reporter,
and banquet hound."

The young reporter's first assignment for the South Bend newspaper
failed to endear him to his editors. Sent to cover the wedding of a member
of the Studebaker family, well known in the community, he returned to the
office with only five lines of news, which, one of his biographers noted, "is
probably just what he thought it was worth." For his next assignment, he
gave a negative review to a show written by the owner of the theater where
it was presented, who also happened to be a major advertiser with the *Times*.

Lardner discovered his true calling with the newspaper in April when
he started covering South Bend's entry in the Central League, a Class B
minor league with teams also in Canton, Dayton, Evansville, Grand Rapids,
Springfield, Terre Haute and Wheeling. In those days, minor leagues were
not directly tied to major-league teams but rather were independent entities.
Players were lionized by local fans as much as today's big leaguers, and
according to baseball historian Bill James, some of the "best players in the
game were in the minor leagues."

The South Bend team's games were played at Spring Brook Park, and
Lardner, newest *Times* reporter on the job, was appointed by the league
president to serve as official scorer. The dollar-a-game salary he received
hardly covered the trouble it caused him. In hopes of impressing major-

league scouts, minor-league ballplayers often pressured the official scorer to rule anything—even an obvious error—as a base hit. With the official scorer's desk just twelve feet from the visiting club's bench, Lardner had several altercations with players.

Writing a story a day during the season, Lardner, while with the *Times*, developed the characteristic style he used in his later work. "Instead of writing a stringy, inning-by-inning account," Donald Edler, Lardner's biographer noted, "he composed his story around a personality or a single dramatic play, and then put into it all the pace and color of a particular game." His own brand of humor also filled those early stories, as Lardner displayed a keen sense of just how far he could go in teasing and tormenting the colorful characters that inhabited America's game at the turn of the twentieth century.

In addition to his duties as a reporter and official scorer, Lardner also found time to further his passion for the game by serving as a scout for South Bend team owners Bert McInerny and Ed Doran. During the winter of 1906 and

Owen "Donie" Bush started as shortstop for the Detroit Tigers from 1908 to 1921. After his playing days were over, he managed several major-league ballclubs and served as president and co-owner of the Indianapolis Indians minor-league team. *Library of Congress.*

1907, Lardner learned that a promising young player on the Dayton team, Owen J. Bush, had been released. Informing McInerny and Doran of Bush's availability, they signed him. Bush, although only five feet, six inches tall and weighing 145 pounds, turned in a stellar performance for the team as its shortstop. Looking for bigger game, Lardner next tried to interest Chicago White Sox owner Charles Comiskey and Chicago Cubs owner Charles Murphy in Bush. The young reporter had met both men at the 1906 World Series between the two clubs, and both "had asked me to keep on the lookout for promising young ball players and to report by wire, collect, if I saw one," Lardner remembered. "I would be financially rewarded if the players I recommended were drafted or bought, and made good."

If he convinced a major-league team to sign Bush, Lardner also stood to receive a cut from the South Bend owners, whose only hope of breaking even during a season came when they possessed a ballplayer good enough—Bush in this case—to elicit an offer from a major-league team before the first day of September, after which Class B players could no longer be bought but were instead subject to the draft. After spending $9.30 in telephone calls and telegrams, Lardner was unsuccessful in his attempts to get a team to sign Bush. Eventually drafted by Detroit, Bush went on to a successful career with the Tigers. After his days as a player ended, Bush managed the Pittsburgh Pirates, the White Sox and the Indianapolis Indians.

Lardner kept busy in the off season by visiting every city in the Central League during the spring of 1907 and reporting on any activity. When Terre Haute traded Buck Weaver to a Little Rock team, Lardner noted that Weaver had been keeping in shape over the winter "by acting as a life-saving line at a Terre Haute skating rink." Upon the hiring of new umpire Ollie Chill from Indianapolis, Lardner informed his readers that the rookie man in blue had "obtained his preliminary training throwing pianos into the second-story windows of flat buildings. During his experience as an umpire, he has been known to pick small disgruntled ball players up by the Adam's apple and toss them to the roof of the grandstand."

In the summer of 1907, Lardner split his time between his passion for baseball and his passion for Ellis Abbott of Goshen, Indiana. The two were introduced to each other while attending a picnic along the St. Joseph River in Niles. His future wife inspired Lardner to write, "The first time I cast my eyes upon young Ellis fair, I thought, 'It's my affinity who's seated over there.'" With Lardner embarking on a sportswriting career, however, the couple endured a long courtship, finally marrying on June 28, 1911.

Lardner's tenure at the *Times* ended in the fall of 1907, when he developed "a desire to quit South Bend and get a job on a paper in Chicago or New York." His wish came true through the aid of an old family friend. Ring and Rex Lardner cleverly timed their vacations to coincide with the World Series between the Cubs and Tigers. While in Chicago, the Lardners stayed with the Jacks family, former friends from Niles. When Ring informed Phil Jacks of his wish for a change, his friend, who knew Hugh S. Fullerton, baseball writer for the *Chicago Examiner*, arranged a meeting between the two for the next day.

After a brief meeting in the *Examiner* offices, the two men retired to a neighborhood bar for a few drinks before the end-of-the-season game between the White Sox and St. Louis Browns. The liquor, said Lardner, "did away with my innate reticence," and he and Fullerton were soon engaged in a friendly discussion about baseball. When the men arrived at the game, Fullerton introduced Lardner to Comiskey and proclaimed,

"I'm going to find a job for this boy in somebody's sporting department. He's been writing baseball on the *South Bend Times* for two years, but he isn't as sappy as that sounds."

Fullerton arranged for Lardner to be seated next to him in the press box when the World Series opened in Chicago at the West Side Ball Park and even traveled with him to Detroit. The series ended with the Cubs sweeping the Tigers in four games. Fullerton introduced Lardner to Frank B. Hutchinson of the *Chicago Inter-Ocean*, and Hutchinson offered him a sportswriting job at $18.50 per week. After Lardner accepted the offer, his new boss asked him how he could manage to living in Chicago on such a small salary. "I can get on the wagon [swear off liquor]," Lardner said. "You can get on the wagon," Hutchinson responded, "but nobody can work for us and stay there."

Lardner's decision to leave South Bend did not sit well with his employers, who realized that they were losing a talented reporter. Fortunately, Lardner's young assistant, J.P. McEvoy, was able to take over his old job. "The real requiem," Lardner said, "was held in the old manse in Niles, Michigan." His mother, who considered Chicago to be "a huge collection of Gomorrahs," arranged for her son's room and board at a respectable woman's home on the city's north side. After a short time, however, Lardner found he could no longer afford this arrangement and moved to a single room on the corner of North State and Goethe Streets.

Although Lardner made it back to the old family home on numerous occasions throughout his life—he provided financial support for his family as his fame grew—the sheltered existence he knew as a youth faded as he dealt with the hard life of a roving reporter and writer. "Small towns are fine to grow up in and a writer finds out a lot of things in small towns he can't learn anywhere else," Lardner later observed. "But it wouldn't be the same as you got older in a small town." Those things he learned while living in a small town, and his experiences as a journalist in South Bend, permeated Lardner's literary life—a career that produced, according to Virginia Woolf, "the best prose that has come our way."

SAVING WASHINGTON

LEW WALLACE AND THE BATTLE OF MONOCACY

Rebel lieutenant general Jubal "Old Jube" Early found himself in an enviable position: he was just a few days' march from what could be one of the most stunning triumphs of the Civil War. In the early summer of 1864, while Robert E. Lee and Ulysses S. Grant were stuck in trench warfare around Petersburg, Virginia, Early and his Army of the Valley had slipped away from the siege and moved into the Shenandoah Valley, successfully cleared it of two Union armies, exacted $220,000 in ransom from Northern cities and even burned the home of the Federal postmaster general. The way was now tantalizingly clear to the heart of the Yankees: Washington, D.C.

The only thing standing between Early's Confederate veterans—whose numbers ranged in panicky estimates from fourteen thousand all to way to twenty-eight thousand—and the Union capital were a handful of novice troops. Commanding these untried soldiers was an officer who had been vilified for his role in the Union near-defeat at the bloody Battle of Shiloh two years before: Major General Lew Wallace of Indiana.

Wallace, commanding the Eighth Army Corps and the Middle Department based in Baltimore—whose job it was to train soldiers, not lead them into battle—knew that a sizeable Rebel force was coming his way. Without any orders from his superiors, Wallace decided to move his small force from Baltimore to the Monocacy River near the town of Frederick, just sixty miles from Washington. It was there on July 9, 1864, that Early and Wallace's forces met. Although the Northern troops repulsed five separate

At the age of thirty-four, Lew Wallace of Indiana received promotion to the rank of major general, the youngest to reach such a status in the Union army. *Library of Congress.*

Rebel charges, they were defeated. However, Wallace and his men did delay Early's march on the capital by one day—enough time for the city to prepare to meet the Confederate threat. Giving orders to collect the bodies of the dead in a burial ground on the battlefield, Wallace proposed a fitting memorial for those who fell: "These men died to save the National Capital, and they did save it."

Who was this man who saved the Union from disaster? A yearning for martial glory had long been a part of Wallace's life. The son of David Wallace, the sixth governor of Indiana, Lew Wallace, as a child growing up in Brookville, had little interest in school; he even ran away from home at one point to serve in the Texas navy during the Texans' struggle for independence from Mexico. Although he studied for a career as an attorney in his father's Indianapolis law office, Wallace failed to pass the bar examination in 1846. (Later in life, he told his wife that the practice of law was "the most detestable of human occupations.") The nineteen-year-old Wallace volunteered for service in the army during the Mexican-American War. He was elected second lieutenant in the First Regiment, Indiana Volunteers, but saw no battle action.

Upon his return from the war, Wallace was admitted to the bar in 1849 and opened a law practice in Covington, where he served two terms as prosecuting attorney. He married Susan Elston on May 6, 1852, and the couple moved in 1853 to Crawfordsville, where Wallace was elected to the state Senate as a Democrat in 1856. Also that year, he organized a military group called the Montgomery Guards. After learning about the French Algerian Zouaves, Wallace converted his company to their system, emulating their colorful uniforms, theatrical drill and commando tactics.

Wallace was ready when hostilities commenced between the North and South with the firing on Fort Sumter on April 12, 1861. In his autobiography, Wallace said he believed that the "conflict would be long and great, but that it would also be crowded with opportunities for distinction not in the least inconsistent with patriotism." The day after the war's outbreak, Wallace visited the offices of Indiana governor Oliver P. Morton, who asked him to become the state's adjutant general. Wallace agreed and became responsible for organizing the Hoosier State's quota of six regiments (4,683 men) for the Union cause.

Just four days after President Abraham Lincoln's call for six regiments from Indiana, Wallace had raised more than twice the number needed. These regiments numbered from the Sixth through the Eleventh in honor of the five Indiana regiments organized during the Mexican-American War. With his task complete, Wallace resigned from his adjutant general post and received command of the Eleventh Indiana Volunteer Infantry Regiment as its colonel.

Wallace's self-proclaimed "love of a military life" next surfaced in a dramatic way. Before leaving Indianapolis for the war, Wallace had his men march to the Indiana Statehouse, where he made them kneel and swear an oath to avenge their comrades whom Wallace believed had been unjustly accused of cowardice by General Zachary Taylor at the Battle of Buena Vista in the Mexican-American War. The stirring scene and oath of "Remember Buena Vista!" caught the state's and the nation's fancy. The influential magazine *Harper's Weekly* produced a full-page illustration of the scene for its readers.

THE ELEVENTH INDIANA VOLUNTEERS SWEARING TO REMEMBER BUENA VISTA, AT INDIANAPOLIS, MAY, 1861.—Sketched by Mr. James F. Gookins.—[See Page 290.]

The Eleventh Indiana Volunteer Infantry Regiment, under the command of Wallace, swears to "Remember Buena Vista!" before a cheering crowd in front of the Indiana Statehouse in Indianapolis, May 1861. *Indiana Historical Society, P0455.*

The Eleventh Indiana was quick to see battle. In June 1861, Wallace and his men surprised Confederate forces in Romney, Virginia, driving them from the town—an operation called "a splendid dash" by President Lincoln. Moving back to the western theater of the war, the regiment participated in the successful campaigns under Grant's leadership to capture Fort Henry and Fort Donelson. In March 1862, at thirty-four years of age, Wallace received promotion to major general—the youngest person to hold that rank in the Union army—and given command of a division. The road to further honor and glory seemed clear. All that changed, however, at the Battle of Shiloh.

On the morning of April 6, 1862, Rebel troops under General Albert Sidney Johnston surprised Grant's army, which was camped at Shiloh Church, just west of the Tennessee River, about twenty miles north of Corinth, Mississippi, and pushed their blue-coated foes all the way to the river's banks. Several miles to the north of the battlefield, Wallace received what were, to him, unclear orders from Grant. Wallace took his command on a confusing march (at one point even finding himself in the rear of the Confederate army) that essentially put his force out of action on the battle's first day.

Wallace and his men, combined with reinforcements brought by Major General Don Carlos Buell, did join other Union soldiers to drive the Confederates from the field on the second day, but at an enormous cost. Of the 100,000 men who participated in the fight, 25,000 were killed or wounded, a number that exceeded all of the United States' combat casualties in its previous wars. Indiana soldiers made up almost one-tenth of the 13,000 Union losses. Wallace's division suffered fewer than 300 casualties. After Shiloh, General Henry Halleck took to the field himself, demoting Grant to second in command.

Debate still rages today about Wallace's action at the battle. The best analysis, to me, came from the Hoosier's former commanding officer, Grant, who theorized that Wallace took the meandering route he did to "come around on the flank or the rear of the enemy, and thus perform an act of heroism that would redound to the credit of his command, as well as to the benefit of his country." At the time, however, Wallace came in for heavy criticism for his tardiness and was eventually stripped of his command. He was informed of his removal by Governor Morton while on leave back home in Indiana. "Somebody in the dark gave me a push," Wallace said later, "and I fell, and fell so far that I could almost see bottom." Wallace, who regarded Halleck—a West Point graduate who was wary of "political" soldiers like Wallace—as being responsible for his removal, returned to his Crawfordsville home to await whatever fate had in store for him.

Wallace was not completely "on the shelf" after the horror of Shiloh. In the late summer of 1862, he was called back into action to help bolster Union defenses around Cincinnati to help thwart an expected Confederate attack. The "turning point," as Wallace termed it, in the reestablishment of his military career occurred on March 12, 1864, when he received orders from the War Department to take command of the Eighth Army Corps, and of the Middle Department, headquartered in Baltimore. "It was President Lincoln's own suggestion—good enough in itself," Wallace wrote of his new assignment in his autobiography. "Then, when I heard that General Halleck had called upon the President, and in person protested against the assignment, there was an added sweetness to it so strong that my disappointment in not being sent to the field was at once and most agreeably allayed." Writing to Major General William Tecumseh Sherman, Halleck lamented the decision to appoint Wallace, saying that it seemed "but little better than murder to give such important commands to such men, yet it seems impossible to prevent it."

General Henry Halleck had little use for "political generals" such as Wallace. For his part, President Abraham Lincoln described Halleck as "little more than a first rate clerk." *Library of Congress.*

Shortly after receiving his orders, Wallace traveled to Washington to meet with Lincoln about his new duties. The president, Wallace recalled later, laid his large hand on his shoulder and told him, "I believed it right to give you a chance, Wallace." At the meeting's conclusion, Lincoln called the Hoosier general back into the room and noted that he had almost forgotten there was an election approaching in Maryland, "but don't *you* forget it."

The election, which involved a constitutional amendment to outlaw slavery, was also the subject of Wallace's subsequent meeting with Secretary of War Edwin Stanton. "It is kindness," Wallace quoted Stanton, "saying it [the election] will be your first trial." Stanton also informed Wallace that the president favored abolition but warned him against the appearance of using the bayonet to sway voters.

With the election set for April 6, 1864, Wallace swung into action. Petitioned by voting precincts to send troops to police the polls, the new commander met with Maryland governor Augustus Bradford. The two came up with a plan whereby Wallace would send the petitions for troops to Bradford, who would then make a written request for the soldiers to Wallace. Troops were eventually dispatched to every doubtful precinct in Maryland and produced the needed results. Wallace noted that in many instances, "the sight of the 'blue-coated hirelings' a mile away, so enraged the Secessionists they refused to go to the polls. In due time, of course, the convention was held, and slavery abolished by formal amendment of the constitution." Wallace's skills in handling his department, however, would soon be put to a sterner test.

In June 1864, with his forces besieged by Grant outside Richmond, Lee concocted a daring plan and entrusted its performance to the hard-charging, sometimes foul-mouthed Early, a veteran of campaigns from First Bull Run through the Wilderness. In his memoirs, Early said that Lee ordered his forces into the Shenandoah Valley "to strike [Union general David] Hunter's force in the rear and, if possible, destroy it; then to move down the valley, cross the Potomac near Leesburg…or at or above Harper's Ferry, as I might find most practicable, and threaten Washington city."

Early and his men set out on their mission on June 13, 1864. The Confederate raid would, Lee hoped, accomplish two things. One, the raid might alarm officials in Washington enough so that they would order troops northward to defend the city, weakening Grant's forces enough to give Lee's army an opportunity to drive them from the Confederate capital. Or, Lee reasoned, the raid might encourage Grant into striking first, perhaps another bloody assault like the one at Cold Harbor, that would reduce his strength enough for the South to strike back. There seemed to be no expectation on Lee's part that

Left: Confederate general Jubal Early had been trained at the U.S. Military Academy before the Civil War and served under Stonewall Jackson early in the conflict. *Library of Congress.*

Right: Following his success in the field as Union commander during the Civil War, Ulysses S. Grant served as president from March 4, 1869, to March 4, 1877. *Library of Congress.*

Early would, in fact, enter Washington. Lee's orders to Early were merely to threaten the city, and when Early suggested to him the idea of capturing the city, Lee said such a thing would be impossible. Lee was almost proven wrong.

By July 1, Early's troops had chased two Union armies—one the aforementioned Hunter and the other commanded by Major General Franz Sigel—out of the Shenandoah Valley. He also plundered Federal stores at Harper's Ferry and extracted $20,000 in ransom from Hagerstown residents and $200,000 from the town of Frederick. The road to Washington seemed clear.

The Union's reaction to this audacious Confederate effort was confused at best; Grant even telegraphed Halleck on July 3 that Early's corps was still near Richmond. One person who did suspect what was happening was Wallace. A day before Grant's message to Halleck in Washington, Wallace had met with John Garrett, president of the Baltimore and Ohio Railroad, at the general's headquarters in Baltimore. Garrett's railroad agents at Cumberland and Harper's Ferry reported the appearance of Rebel forces.

Without any orders from Washington, and without at first informing his superiors, Wallace acted. He did so even though he knew that his enemies, particularly General Halleck, might use any failure on his part as an excuse to be rid of him once and for all. In asking himself what the Confederates' objective could be, Wallace could come up with only one to justify the risks involved: Washington. On the night of July 4, he and an aide took a train to Monocacy Junction (also called Frederick Junction) to survey the lay of the land. At this point, the Georgetown Pike to Washington and the National Road to Baltimore both crossed the Monocacy River, as did the Baltimore and Ohio Railroad. In deciding whether to make his stand at Monocacy, Wallace ran over in his mind all of the consequences the fall of the Union capital might entail. To him, "they grouped themselves into a kind of horrible schedule," which included the following:

> At the navy-yard there were ships making and repairing, which, with the yard itself, would be given over to flames.
>
> In the treasury department there were millions of bonds printed, and other millions signed and ready for issuance—how many millions I did not know.
>
> There were storehouses in the city filled with property of all kinds, medical, ordnance, commissary, quartermaster, the accumulation of years, without which the war must halt, if not stop for good an all.
>
> Then I thought of the city, the library, the beautiful capital, all under menace…of Louis Napoleon and Gladstone hastening to recognize the Confederacy as a nation.

There was one thought that hardened Wallace's resolve to hold his ground against any attack. It was, he said, "an apparition of President Lincoln, cloaked and hooded, stealing like a malefactor from the back door of the White House just as some gray-garbed Confederate brigadier burst in the front door." In deciding to stay and meet the foe with his "raw and untried" 2,300-man force, Wallace hoped that he would be able to make the enemy disclose the size of his force and his intended objective. If it was Washington, as Wallace feared, the Union general wanted to delay the Rebels enough to give Grant the time to send troops north to reinforce the city.

Early's and Wallace's forces first met on July 7 just outside Frederick. This initial skirmish went to Wallace, as the Confederates withdrew near nightfall.

The Union commander's message to Halleck in Washington was optimistic, stating that the Confederates "were handsomely repulsed." Things seemed to be going Wallace's way when, that night, his forces were bolstered by veteran soldiers of the Third Division of the Sixth Corps under Brigadier General James Ricketts, which had been sent north by Grant. By the night of July 8, however, Wallace had pulled his men out of Frederick and made his stand east of the Monocacy River, positioning themselves at both turnpike bridges, the railroad bridge and several fords.

On the morning of July 9, the main body of Early's force, which doubled Wallace's numbers, hurled itself at the Federal troops. The battle raged on for nearly six hours; Union troops withstood numerous attacks before retreating toward Baltimore. The fierce fighting and heroic resistance offered by the Union troops are best highlighted in the fact that two of them—Corporal Alexander Scott and First Lieutenant George E. Davis, both from the Tenth Regiment of Vermont Volunteers—were awarded the Medal of Honor for their actions at Monocacy. The Federals lost 98 killed, 594 wounded and 1,188 missing in the battle. Early estimated his killed and wounded at 600 to 900 men. Wallace reported to Halleck that he was "retreating with a foot-sore, battered, and half-demoralized column"—not a report to inspire the confidence of his superiors.

Despite the pessimistic tone of Wallace's battle report, he and his men had accomplished their task: they had delayed Early's march on Washington by one full day. Early resumed his march to the city on July 10 and reached the outskirts of the city the next day. He was too late; Grant had sent enough men north to beat back the Confederates. Even though Early did attempt an attack on the city on July 12, he knew he was too late. He began the trek back south but kept his bravado intact, telling Major Kyd Douglas, "Major, we haven't taken Washington, but we've scared Abe Lincoln like hell!"

In his memoirs, Early blamed earlier battle losses for his decision not to engage in a full-scale attack on the capital. He noted that fighting at Harper's Ferry, Maryland Heights and Monocacy had reduced his infantry forces to eight thousand in number. Those troops left were "greatly exhausted by the last two days' marching, some having fallen by sunstroke, and not more than one-third of my force could have been carried into action." The Confederate army retreated across the Potomac River at White's Ford and returned to Virginia.

Wallace initially received little credit for his actions in delaying Early's march on the capital. In fact, on July 11, he was relieved of command of

Writing to his wife, Susan, after his victory at Fort Donelson, Wallace said he never "heard music as fascinating and grand as that of battle." *Library of Congress.*

the Middle Department by Major General E.O.C. Ord. That same day, an obviously upset Wallace wired Secretary Stanton, "Does General Ord report to me, or am I to understand that he relieves me from command of the Department. If so, what am I to do?"

The tide soon turned on Wallace's behalf as officials realized that his daring stand at Monocacy had saved the capital from disaster. In a July 24 letter to his friend B.J. Lossing, Wallace reported that Stanton had complimented him on the Battle of Monocacy, saying it was "timely, well-delivered, well-managed, and saved Washington. The stories about my removal are all bosh. On the contrary, you may set me **down** as on the *rise*." Wallace was right; just four days later, he received orders from the War Department, under the direction of President Lincoln, to resume command of the Eighth Army Corps and the Middle Department. Writing to his brother later that fall, Wallace boasted that he could say what no other general officer in the army could—that a defeat did more for him than all the victories he had been involved in.

Wallace's gallant stand at Monocacy may have faded from people's memories as his other subsequent accomplishments took center stage. But no less an authority than Grant fully appreciated Wallace's role on that critical day. Writing about the Battle of Monocacy in his classic memoirs, Grant noted the following: "If Early had been but one day earlier he might have entered the capital before the arrival of the reinforcements I had sent. Whether the delay caused by the battle amounted to a day or not, General Wallace contributed on this occasion, by the defeat of the troops under him, a greater benefit to the cause than often falls to the lot of a commander of an equal force to render by means of a victory."

"THE LAST ENEMY IS DESTROYED"

MAY WRIGHT SEWALL AND SPIRITUALISM

In the summer of 1918, Booth Tarkington, enjoying the season at his home in Kennebunkport, Maine, received in the mail an invitation from an old friend from Indianapolis, who was also in Maine, to meet and discuss a manuscript the friend had written. In the letter, the friend, May Wright Sewall, did not indicate the subject of her writing, but knowing of her previous work in Indiana, Tarkington assumed that the book would be "something educational." When he finally received the manuscript, the Hoosier writer was astonished to discover "that for more than twenty years this academic-liberal of a thousand human activities…had been really living not with the living, so to put it."

Writing her with his initial assessment of the work, Tarkington told Sewall that he had read the manuscript "very carefully and with an ever increasing interest." Calling the book "unique," he added that it proved "its over absolute sincerity from the *first*, and beyond question; total strangers to you, personally, would recognize that." Sewall's manuscript, eventually published by the Bobbs-Merrill Company of Indianapolis just two months before her death in July 1920 as *Neither Dead Nor Sleeping*, detailed her extensive experiences in the shadowy world of spiritualism—the belief in the possibility of the living communicating with the dead.

Sewall's communion with the deceased, including extensive conversations with her late husband, Theodore, shocked many who knew the no-nonsense teacher, suffragette and peace advocate. This proponent of spiritualism had played a leading role in helping to establish such Indianapolis institutions as the Girls' Classical School, the Indianapolis Woman's Club, the Contemporary Club, the Art Association of Indianapolis and the Indianapolis Propylaeum. She also worked tirelessly to promote rights for women in the United States—and around the world—during the late nineteenth and early twentieth centuries, serving as an invaluable ally to such national suffrage leaders as Susan B. Anthony and Elizabeth Cady Stanton. Sewall also gave the women's movement an international focus through her pioneering involvement with the International Council of Women and the National Council of Women. In addition to her work on behalf of suffrage, Sewall had been a leader in the American peace movement, serving as a delegate on Henry Ford's ill-fated peace mission to end World War I.

Hoosier author Booth Tarkington twice won the Pulitzer Prize for his novels—in 1919 for *The Magnificent Ambersons* and in 1922 for *Alice Adams*. *Library of Congress.*

Anton Scherrer, a columnist for the *Indianapolis Times*, said that nothing "rocked the foundations of Indianapolis quite as much" as had the appearance of Sewall's publication, because nobody in her old hometown knew about her contacts with the spirit world. In fact, only a dozen or so people knew about this side of her life. During Sewall's communications with her departed husband, he had warned her, she told a reporter from the *Indianapolis Star*, not to relate them "to the world until she had them in such form the world could understand them." Also, those to whom she related her experiences often expressed the belief that Sewall suffered from a mental delusion. Perhaps realizing that she would be ridiculed by many for her otherworldly experiences, which first occurred in 1897, she decided to relate her spiritualist story to the world only when "extreme feebleness" had taken her once and for all out of public affairs.

Sewall began her commune with the spirits during a visit to a spiritualist camp meeting in Lily Dale, New York, in 1897. The seeds for her communications with the deceased, however, had been planted a few years before during some of the darkest days of her life. A fortnight before her husband's death from tuberculosis on December 23, 1895, he had told her that his death was inevitable. "I wish now only to say that if I discover that

May Wright Sewall's second husband, Theodore, graduated from Harvard University and later served as head of the Indianapolis Classical School. *Robert W. Sewall.*

I survive death," said Theodore Sewall, "the first thing I shall do will be to ascertain whether or not Jesus ever returned to earth after His crucifixion. You know we have not believed it; but, if I find that He did return to His disciples, I shall do nothing else until I shall have succeeded in returning to you, unless before that time, you have come to me."

Although her husband's memory remained fresh in Sewall's mind during the next few years, she claimed to have forgotten his deathbed promise to communicate with her from the spirit world. In fact, when some Indianapolis friends advised Sewall to visit a local medium in order to see and talk again with her husband, the proposal shocked her. "It seemed to me grossly to violate both reason and delicacy," she said. Instead of taking them up on their offer, Sewall continued to give her time to her school and work with both the National and International Council of Women. During a speaking engagement in Nova Scotia in June 1897, she received an invitation to give a talk at a "Woman's Day" program at what she later learned was a spiritualist camp in Lily Dale. "I had held myself so aloof from all means of information about spiritualism," she said, "that I did not know there were such camps."

Sewall arrived at Lily Dale's assembly grounds on August 9, 1897, and was greeted by the chairman of the press committee for the National American Woman Suffrage Association, who asked her if she wished to tour the facility and be introduced to some of the famous mediums gathered there for the meeting. "I told her," said Sewall, "that I did not wish to meet any 'medium' however 'famous'; that to me the word was offensive, being synonymous in my opinion, with the words, deceiver, pretender, charlatan and ignoramus." Although her audience the next day proved to be "attentive, responsive and sympathetic," Sewall wanted nothing more than to depart the place for her next speaking engagement at Chautauqua, New York.

A series of unexpected difficulties, however, caused Sewall to stay over at Lily Dale for a time. Giving in to a "compelling impulse which I scarcely realized until I acted upon it," she participated in a sitting with a famous independent slate writer, a medium who used slates to convey messages from the spirits to their intended recipients. During her meeting with the slate writer, Sewall claimed that the blank slates never left her possession, but when she returned with them to her hotel, she discovered that they were covered with "clear and legible writing" and contained "perfectly coherent, intelligent and characteristic replies to questions which I had written upon bits of paper that had not passed out of my hands."

Through this experience, Sewall said she had acquired "actual knowledge, if not of immortality, at least of a survival of death—I had learned that the last enemy is destroyed, in that he can destroy neither being nor identity, nor continuity of relationship." Through subsequent sittings with slate writers, trance readers, a trumpet medium and other psychics, Sewall communicated with several of her deceased loved ones, including her husband, father, mother, half sister, great-grandfather, niece and two sisters-in-law.

As she became more attuned to the spirit world, Sewall managed to communicate with her husband herself through automatic writing. Equipped with only a tablet and pencil, she sat in her library and her husband's spirit would guide her hand to produce written answers to her questions about life beyond the grave. These amazing messages, she later told the *Indianapolis Star*, came to her as impressions on her mind.

Sewall noted that the experience was as though she received "a blow on the brain—not physically of course—but clear and distinct and without warning. And in an instant comes a complete train of thought—swift—immediate—not arrived at by the slow and ordinary sequence of ideas—a complete train of thought solving some heretofore unsolvable riddle of the universe." These thoughts—an extensive series of lectures from Theodore Sewall on how spirits return and communicate with the living—could not have come from her own mind, she insisted, for they often concerned themes that she had never imagined in her entire life.

Sewall's remarkable account of her communications with the spirit world became known to the living through the unstinting efforts of an Indiana writer who had his own experience with unexplained phenomena: Booth Tarkington. When he was fourteen years old and living in Indianapolis, Tarkington discovered that his sister, Hauté, had psychic powers. The Tarkington family hosted séances at its home that drew such distinguished visitors as James Whitcomb Riley. Although Hauté's powers faded away after her marriage, her devoted brother remained convinced of the reality of his experiences. Throughout his life, noted Tarkington biographer James Woodress, the writer "was tolerant of other persons' alleged supersensory experience." When Sewall approached him for assistance in finding a publisher for her spiritualist manuscript, Tarkington proved eager to help.

In the fall of 1918, Tarkington had a stenographer make a copy of Sewall's manuscript to present to possible publishers. He wrote her that he needed to find a firm willing not only to print the book but also to effectively promote it. "I assure you that I will do everything within my power not only to get it printed," he said, "but to get it 'pushed'!" Tarkington reiterated his belief that Sewall's manuscript stood as a "unique document with the air of a classic in human experience."

By March 1919, Tarkington had decided to place the manuscript with the Bobbs-Merrill Company, which could trace its roots in Indianapolis back to the 1850s and was the publisher for such Hoosier literary lions as Riley, George Ade, Meredith Nicholson and Maurice Thompson. Tarkington passed along Sewall's manuscript to Bobbs-Merrill with the understanding that he would write an introduction for the book. He did warn Sewall that a decision on whether to publish her work might take some time.

Tarkington's warning proved to be prophetic. During the spring and summer, he exchanged a series of letters with Sewall discussing the lack of a decision from Bobbs-Merrill on the book. Although the firm's literary adviser and trade editor, Hewitt H. Howland, had told Tarkington he was in favor of accepting the book, and Tarkington wrote to Sewall that he was tempted to push the firm about the manuscript, he feared doing so because a "very little push upon a publisher sometimes turns him aside from the right path." A final decision on the manuscript depended on the opinion of William C. Bobbs, the company's president, "and *that* must take its own time not ours!" said Tarkington. By the end of July, Tarkington's patience had been tried enough for him to suggest to Sewall that she write a note to Howland "and hint that you can wait no longer."

Sometime in August, Bobbs-Merrill finally agreed to publish Sewall's spiritualist book. One of the reasons for the firm's acceptance might have been its eagerness to add Tarkington to its list of authors. For his part, Tarkington continued to advise the suffragist, sending her suggestions on how to conduct contract negotiations with the Indianapolis publishing firm. "I am sure he [Howland] will be fair and the terms will be customary—it is always about the same thing: 10% gross, I suppose, on sales up to 10,000 and 15% thereafter—some such arrangement," he told Sewall. "I should let him propose the terms and, if they are like this, accept at once." The Hoosier writer went on to try to convince Sewall not to believe that his "small" contribution had induced Bobbs-Merrill to accept the book. Perhaps his efforts on her behalf did pique the firm's interest in reviewing the manuscript, but it was the work "itself, and nothing else whatever, that has brought them to their favorable decision."

During her exchange of letters with Tarkington about her manuscript, the seventy-five-year-old Sewall, who had been in ill health, had been making plans to leave the East Coast and return to live in Indianapolis. She had even written to her old suffragist friend Grace Julian Clarke to seek advice on possible places for her to stay. Clarke wrote back expressing her delight at Sewall's decision to live again in Indianapolis but reported that the three places she had in mind as possible locations for Sewall to take up residence were unavailable. Undeterred by Clarke's bad news about lodgings for her, Sewall remained resolved to return to Indianapolis, the scene of many of the triumphs and tragedies in her life. Writing from the Aloha Rest Convalescent Home in Winthrop Highlands, Massachusetts, she expressed to Howland, the editor for her book, her gratitude for accepting her manuscript, adding that it pleased her to have the book published in the city where many of the experiences took place.

Although Sewall consented to Howland's request to shorten the second part of the book, she did ask him one favor. She indicated that she was quite anxious to have the book come out as soon as possible because numerous publishing firms, including the most conservative ones, were issuing books on spiritualism in order to take advantage of the huge surge in interest in the subject from families who had lost loved ones during World War I. "The war has terribly increased the number of bereaved and bleeding hearts and often the skepticism of the intellect can be broken down only through the agony of a yearning heart," she said. "I, who *have* suffered, want to help those who do suffer."

In early October 1919, Sewall finally returned to Indianapolis, taking up residence at a convalescent home at 1732 North Illinois Street. Although so ill with heart disease that she had trouble breathing and had to be propped up in bed by pillows, Sewall, looked

Portrait of Sewall used by the Bobbs-Merrill Company to promote her book *Neither Dead Nor Sleeping. Lilly Library, Indiana University, Bloomington, Indiana.*

after by some of her former students at the Girls' Classical School, managed to make corrections on galley proofs of her book. In spite of her illness, she remained confident about the worth of her manuscript. "I think I never did a better piece of proof reading—and I am perfectly delighted with the book," she told Howland in December. "I *know* it will have an ultimate great success." Sewall's confidence may have been inspired by the rapport she had established with her editor. She apologized to Howland for hindering the work on her book because of her illness but promised to keep herself well enough to proof as fast as it arrived.

As winter turned into spring and her book remained unpublished, Sewall began to get apprehensive about the future. "I beg you to believe," she said in a dictated letter to Howland, "that I am distressed at feeling the need of troubling you, but I have been very ill for several weeks with the prospect of continuing so, or worse; and I am beginning to be very anxious about the possibility of holding out until my book is out." She went on to say that she did not know if he could do anything to hurry the process but was sure that if "you could know my distressing situation you would be sympathetically anxious to try and hurry it." By the time Howland could present Sewall with a complimentary copy of her book on May 8, she had been moved from her Illinois Street residence to room 131 at St. Vincent's Hospital.

Bobbs-Merrill placed its considerable promotional muscle squarely behind *Neither Dead Nor Sleeping*. Calling the work "The Wonder Book of the Ages" and labeling its author "one of the best known among the pioneer progressive women of the country," the firm issued a first printing of three thousand copies and promoted it to book dealers as "a sure-fire seller from the start. It's the kind the dealer will take home and read and reread himself!"

The Indianapolis company had Sewall autograph copies of the book, which sold for three dollars per copy, to be sent to influential literary editors representing such publications as the *Literary Digest*, *Publishers Weekly* and *Booklist*, as well as newspapers in New York, Chicago, Los Angeles and San Francisco. She also prepared signed copies for such influential figures as William Randolph Hearst and his wife. These promotional efforts paid off; Howland reported to Sewall that ten to twelve newspapers had printed full-page stories on the book, and as of early June, one-third of the first printing of three thousand had been sold.

To help ease the reader into the story of Sewall's astonishing experiences, Tarkington had contributed a compelling and open-minded introduction for *Neither Dead Nor Sleeping*. In reading Sewall's story, Tarkington said it seemed to him that her struggle to cure her illness and make herself a proper messenger for the dead were recorded not as a person living in the modern world but as "some medieval penitent, feeding upon snow by day and lying prayerful upon a bed of cinders at night, seeking to become a spirit." Considering the validity of Sewall's spiritualist beliefs, Tarkington had three possible explanations for her story: Sewall was hallucinating her experiences; the communications from the dead were really the work of "an inner self of hers, sometimes called a subconscious"; or the communications were, as Sewall believed them to be, actually from the deceased. For Tarkington, the truth of the matter rested somewhere between the second and third explanations.

Many reviewers echoed Tarkington's sympathetic treatment of Sewall's book. Writing for the *Chicago Tribune*, Elia W. Peattie claimed that the book had been written in "good faith" by a "gentlewoman of high veracity." The author had found, Peattie added, an "escape from illness and sorrow, and there remains but to extend to her sincere and deeply felt congratulations." Reviewing several books on psychic experiences for the *New York Evening Post*, J. Keith Torbert wrote that both for those who believe and for those who scoff at spiritualism Sewall's book "has essentials to reveal." *Neither Dead Nor Sleeping* had, Torbert added, something that raised it above the ordinary. "This is the very human touch to the writing," he wrote. "The strong, admirable character of Mrs. Sewall appears on every page." Sewall's work even received a positive notice in the *New York Times Book Review*. In reviewing eleven books that discussed the question of what happens after a person dies, the *Review* highlighted Sewall's as "one of the most striking—amazing is hardly too strong a word."

These vindications of her work came as Sewall, now seventy-six years old, lay gravely ill in her room at St. Vincent's Hospital, where she finally died at 11:15 p.m. on July 22, 1920. The *Indianapolis Star* reported that her advanced age, taken in connection "with a gradual physical decline manfesting [*sic*] itself in the last three months convinced her physicians some time ago that her recovery was impossible." After funeral services at All Souls Unitarian Church, overseen by Reverend S.C. Wicks, May was buried alongside her beloved husband, Theodore, at Crown Hill Cemetery. In the death of May Wright Sewall, the *Indianapolis News* noted on its editorial page, the world lost a citizen. Throughout her life, "Mrs. Sewall possessed the faculty of transmitting her boundless enthusiasm and her original ideas to the world around her. One could not slumber in her presence for her vitality was contagious."

THE SPEECH

ROBERT F. KENNEDY
AND INDIANAPOLIS

T he City of Indianapolis's parks and recreation department is responsible for administrating nearly two hundred properties stretching over more than eleven thousand acres in the central Indiana community. One of these properties, the Doctor Martin Luther King Jr. Park at 1702 North Broadway Street on the city's near north side, has within its fourteen acres the usual recreational components for an urban park: a basketball court, a playground, a softball field, picnic shelters and an outdoor pool. As Center Township residents while away the hours at play, their eyes are no doubt sometimes drawn to one of the park's most intriguing features, a sculpture titled *A Landmark for Peace*, created by the late Indiana artist Greg Perry and placed in the park in 1995.

The memorial, which is located at the park's south end, features two curved panels facing across from each other. Near the top of each panel is a figure of a man with an arm and hand outstretched toward, but failing to touch, the other. The men depicted in the sculpture, neither of whom is alive to help bridge the gap that still exists today, are the slain civil rights leader Dr. King and the former junior U.S. senator from the state of New York Robert F. Kennedy. By chance and the vagaries of a political campaign, the two are forever bound together in the park, as well as in Indiana and American history.

The predominantly African American crowd that gathered at Seventeenth and Broadway Streets for an outdoor rally on a cold and windy evening on April 4, 1968, appeared to be in a festive mood. And

Robert F. Kennedy and Martin Luther King Jr. reach out to each other in the *Landmark for Peace* memorial sculpture designed and executed by the late artist Greg Perry. *Photo by David Turk.*

why not? Those milling about the Broadway Christian Center's outdoor basketball court—an audience estimated at numbering anywhere from one thousand to three thousand in size—would be among the first people in the Hoosier State to hear from a newly declared presidential candidate, Robert Kennedy, who had announced his run for the Democratic Party's nomination for president on March 16. With his late arrival in the race for the nomination, Kennedy had decided to take his case directly to the people. "Our strategy is to change the rules of nominating a president," noted Adam Walinsky, Kennedy's chief speechwriter. "We're going to do it a new way. In the streets."

Kennedy had selected Indiana as his first test before Democratic voters. In the nineteenth state's May 7 primary, he faced two challengers, Indiana governor Roger D. Branigin, running as a favorite son, and U.S. senator Eugene McCarthy, whose strong showing in the New Hampshire primary against incumbent Lyndon B. Johnson had helped to convince Johnson—along with Kennedy's entrance into the race—to abandon his reelection effort. At the end of a March 31 speech to the nation in which he had announced a halt to the bombing of North Vietnam, Johnson stunned everyone by stating, "I shall not seek, and I will not accept, the nomination of my party for another term as your President."

Those who waited for long hours huddled against the cold to hear Kennedy speak would long remember what they heard. As volunteers worked at nearby tables to register voters, a band played and spectators waved banners and signs touting Kennedy's candidacy, two sixteen-year-old North Central High School students, Mary Evans and Altha Cravey, milled about with the rest of the audience, who were, as one participant described it, "packed in like sardines." Like many young people during that political season, Evans and Cravey had become transfixed by the antiwar candidacy of McCarthy, the Minnesota senator who had decided to take on Johnson to protest America's involvement in Vietnam. Inspired by their growing disgust with the war and McCarthy's commitment to ending the conflict, the local students had volunteered to work for the senator's campaign in Indiana. Despite their allegiance to McCarthy, both, because of their keen interest in politics and public policy, wanted to hear what Kennedy had to say. Neither had heard the news that King had been killed.

There were some in the throng, however, who had grown tired of the choices offered by America's two political parties and were looking for more radical change. Some black activists had heard about King's death and were gathering support in the African American community for violent action. William Crawford, later a longtime Indiana legislator from Indianapolis, was at the time of Kennedy's appearance a member of an organization known as the Radical Action Program. He and his friends were very close, he recalled, to resorting to violence as a way to register their grief and rage at the loss of the civil rights leader. One estimate had close to two hundred militants sprinkled throughout the crowd. Those responsible for local arrangements for the speech, including respected Black Power leader Charles "Snooky" Hendricks, grew so fearful that Kennedy's life might be in danger that they recruited people to check the area for possible assassins.

Before traveling to Indianapolis, Kennedy had made two other campaign stops that day, one at the University of Notre Dame in South Bend and another at Ball State University in Muncie. During a question-and-answer session following his Ball State speech, a young black man had asked the candidate whether Kennedy could justify his belief in the good faith of white people toward minorities. The candidate answered that most people in the country wanted to do "the decent and the right thing."

Kennedy waves to the crowd gathered to hear his speech at Ball State University's Men's Gym on April 4, 1968. The senator's wife, Ethel, can be seen at the rear of the stage. *George T. Yeamans Collection, Archives and Special Collections Research Center, Bracken Library, Ball State University.*

As Kennedy boarded the plane for Indianapolis to formally open his campaign headquarters on East Washington Street and to make an appearance at the outdoor rally in the heart of the city's African American community, Marshall Hanley, one of his key supporters in Delaware County, informed him that King had been gunned down on the balcony of the Lorraine Motel in Memphis, Tennessee. King had traveled to Memphis to offer his support for the city's striking black sanitation workers and their attempts to organize a union. After arriving at Indianapolis's Weir Cook Airport, Kennedy learned that the Nobel Prize–winning activist had died. Thinking back to the answer he had given at Ball State, a distraught Kennedy told a *Newsweek* reporter that it grieved him that he "just told that kid this and then walk out and find that some white man had just shot their spiritual leader."

Kennedy decided to cancel his stop at his campaign headquarters but did proceed on to Seventeenth and Broadway as planned. However, he sent his wife, Ethel, on ahead to the Marott Hotel on North Meridian Street. After a brief statement on King's death to the press assembled at the airport, Kennedy climbed into a car that would take him to the rally, jotting down some notes on what he might say on the back of an envelope. John Bartlow Martin, an Indianapolis native and close adviser to Kennedy during the campaign for the Indiana primary, had also returned to the Marott from dinner. He and Kennedy speechwriter Jeff Greenfield were to work on potential statements for Kennedy to deliver on the tragedy. When he returned to the hotel, Martin saw a local police inspector parked at the curb. He went up to the car and asked the officer if the candidate should go ahead and address the crowd. "He said, with a fervor I imagine was rare in him, 'I sure hope he does. If he doesn't, there'll be hell to pay,'" Martin remembered.

Arriving at the rally, Kennedy, wearing a black overcoat once belonging to his brother John, climbed onto a flatbed truck located in a paved parking lot near the Broadway Christian Center's basketball court. After asking for those waving signs and banners to put them down, he informed them that King had been killed. The audience, which had been anticipating a raucous political event and for the most part had been unaware of the shooting, responded to the announcement with gasps, shrieks and cries of "No! No!" Tom Keating, a police reporter for the *Indianapolis Star*, had raced to the scene with two policemen. He noted that the crowd reacted to the news almost like "a wounded animal" and called the event one of the most "supercharged" he had ever witnessed.

Facing the now stunned and disbelieving audience, some of whom were weeping at their loss, Kennedy gave an impassioned, extemporaneous, nearly six-minute speech on the need for compassion in the face of violence that has gone down in history as one of the great addresses in the modern era. A New York journalist close to Kennedy observed that the candidate "gave a talk that all his skilled speech writers working together could not have surpassed." John Lewis, a seasoned veteran of the civil rights movement who helped organize the rally, recalled that when Kennedy spoke, the crowd hung on his every word. "It didn't matter that he was white or rich or a Kennedy," said Lewis. "At this moment he was just a human being, just like all of us, and he spoke that way."

To help try to explain the terrible tragedy, Kennedy recalled the words of Aeschylus, the Greek tragedian whose words from *Agamemnon* had comforted him following the assassination of his brother, President John F. Kennedy: "He [Aeschylus] once wrote: 'Even in our sleep, pain which cannot forget falls drop by drop upon the heart, until, in our own despair, against our will, comes wisdom

Kennedy informs the crowd gathered for a political rally at Seventeenth and Broadway Streets in Indianapolis that civil rights activist King had been shot and killed earlier that evening in Memphis, Tennessee, April 4, 1968. Indianapolis Recorder *Collection, Indiana Historical Society.*

through the awful grace of God.'" He went on to attempt to calm the crowd's growing anger about King's killing with these words:

> *What we need in the United States is not division; what we need in the United States is not hatred; what we need in the United States is not violence or lawlessness; but love and wisdom, and compassion toward one another, and a feeling of justice toward those who still suffer within our country, whether they be white or they be black....*
>
> *We can do well in this country. We will have difficult times; we've had difficult times in the past; we will have difficult times in the future. It is not the end of violence; it is not the end of lawlessness; it is not the end of disorder....*
>
> *But the vast majority of white people and the vast majority of black people in this country want to live together, want to improve the quality of our life, and want justice for all human beings who abide in our land.*

Let us dedicate ourselves to what the Greeks wrote so many years ago: to tame the savageness of man and to make gentle the life of this world.
Let us dedicate ourselves to that, and say a prayer for our country and for our people.

The news of King's violent death at the hands of a white gunman, James Earl Ray, had sparked outrage and violence across the country. Black activist Stokely Carmichael told a crowd in New York, "Go home and get a gun! When the white man comes he is coming to kill you. I don't want any black blood in the street. Go home and get you a gun and then come back because I got me a gun." Some African Americans took Carmichael's words to heart, as riots exploded in several cities, including Washington, D.C. Regular army troops were called into action by President Johnson to bring the situation under control. But in Indianapolis, the crowd at Seventeenth and Broadway had taken Kennedy's words to heart and had quietly left the rally and returned home. "We walked away in pain but not with a sense of revenge," said Crawford. There were no riots in the Circle City.

Kennedy's remarkable speech marked just the beginning of a whirlwind time in Indiana. "It was perhaps the most exciting month of politics ever in this city and state," noted Keating, who later became a columnist for the *Star*. For most of April and early May, the eyes of the nation turned to the Hoosier State. Reporters and television correspondents from around the country flocked to Indiana to report on what Kennedy and his staff hoped would be a series of primary victories in the senator's effort to capture the 1,312 delegates needed to win the Democratic presidential nomination.

In deciding to make the Indiana primary his first test before the voters, Kennedy hoped that the nineteenth state might provide the same validation to his presidential ambitions as West Virginia had done for his brother in his primary battle with Hubert Humphrey in 1960, removing the taint that no Roman Catholic could be elected president. "Indiana is the ballgame," Kennedy told Martin. "This is my West Virginia." In his campaign literature and rallies before Hoosier voters, Kennedy emphasized that Indiana had the opportunity, with its decision in the Democratic primary, to once again, as it had in the past, play a vital role in the country's presidential contest. "Indiana can help choose a president," Kennedy emphasized again and again in his speeches.

Kennedy hoped to gain enough of a mandate in Indiana to knock McCarthy out of the race for good. Because he could not pick up enough delegates from primary states to win the nomination, Kennedy also

"The youth of our nation are the clearest mirror of our performance."

Kennedy

Brochure distributed by the thousands in the Hoosier State by the Kennedy campaign during the 1968 Indiana primary. *Author Collection.*

wanted to have enough strong showings to impress the heads of city and state Democratic organizations, such as Chicago mayor Richard Daley, who controlled most delegates at the convention through caucuses and state conventions. Kennedy wanted to prove to these party stalwarts that he could attract the support of not just African Americans and college students but also poorer, white voters worried about violence in their communities and fearful of the gains made by African Americans in civil rights and equal access. This was the "white backlash" vote that George Wallace, the segregationist governor of Alabama, had depended on when he captured about 30 percent of the Democratic vote in the 1964 Indiana presidential primary (Indiana governor Matthew E. Welsh, running as a stand-in for Johnson, won the primary with 376,023 votes to Wallace's 172,646). Wallace had run particularly strong in the northwest section of the state in the steel towns of Hammond and Gary and garnered a majority in both Lake and Porter Counties.

Several Kennedy advisers cautioned him against entering the Indiana primary. They saw the state as too conservative, pointing to the strength of the Ku Klux Klan in the state during the 1920s, the fact that John Kennedy had run more than 200,000 votes behind Republican Richard Nixon in the 1960 presidential election in Indiana and Wallace's strong showing in parts of Indiana in the 1964 primary. Kennedy's antiwar views would also clash with Hoosiers' political views, as Indianapolis was home to the national headquarters of the American Legion and the place where Robert Welch Jr. founded the ultraconservative John Birch Society on December 9, 1958, to fight Communist infiltration of the American government.

Venturing into such foreign territory seemed to be a daunting task for both Kennedy's mainly East Coast staff and the media that reported on the campaign. Jules Witcover, who covered every presidential campaign since the early 1960s, recalled being put off by Indianapolis being home to two huge war memorials (the Indiana War Memorial and the Soldiers and Sailors Monument). He spoke the feelings of many national media figures about Indiana in 1968 when he commented, "Were a Martian to land his flying saucer in Monument Circle, he might well take one look, climb back in and beat a fast retreat."

Pondering all the obstacles facing the Kennedy campaign in Indiana, Martin, the author of a well-regarded history of the state, believed Branigin might well win the primary, with Kennedy's best chance to come in second, ahead of McCarthy. The rest of the senator's campaign staff was also pessimistic about their candidate's chances. Echoing Martin's prediction, they attempted to lower expectations by telling anyone who would listen that they did not expect to win but just hoped to run even with the governor. Kennedy's late start and the chaotic nature of the campaign might have prompted the staff's doubts. "The 'smooth-running, well oiled Kennedy machine' got to be an office joke very quickly," said Frank Mankiewicz,

Kennedy's press assistant. Kennedy himself had no illusions about what faced him in Indiana, as well as other primaries to come in states such as Nebraska, Oregon, California, South Dakota and New York. Warned by his advisers that entering the Indiana primary would be a gamble, he replied, "The whole campaign is a gamble."

In addition to showcasing such national political figures as Kennedy and McCarthy, the Indiana presidential primary shone a spotlight on some fascinating Hoosier politicians, especially Branigin, a Harvard-educated lawyer from Franklin, Indiana. An engaging, witty speaker with an encyclopedic knowledge of the state's history, Branigin had initially agreed to run as a stand-in for President Johnson in the primary. With Johnson's announcement that he would not seek or accept his party's nomination for president, a stunned Branigin nevertheless decided to remain in the race as a favorite-son candidate. He hoped to win some influence for Indiana's sixty-three delegates at the Democratic convention in Chicago, slated to be held in August 1968.

McCarthy and his campaign never seemed to hit their stride in Indiana. One key McCarthy staff member called his time in the state a "frustrating, painful experience, lacking the spontaneity of New Hampshire and the organization and enthusiasm of Wisconsin." Workers had to endure poor press coverage, ineffective cooperation with local supporters and a pending strike by telephone installers that hampered the campaign's communication efforts. Those who canvassed the state seeking votes on McCarthy's behalf were usually met with blank stares and the question: "McCarthy who?"

Focusing on appearances in small communities, McCarthy encountered small crowds and appeared uncomfortable connecting with Hoosiers. He seemed put off by what he called "a rather general defensiveness in Indiana against outsiders. In northern Indiana…people seemed worried about the prospect of being taken over by Chicago. In the south, they were threatened by Kentucky, in the west, by Illinois, in the east, by Ohio. It was as though in Indiana they have to think Indiana for fear that if they do not it will be absorbed by the outside world." Erratic scheduling that made him late for some appearances and miss out on large crowds waiting for him in others did not help matters. Later, McCarthy summed up his unease while campaigning by noting that he kept hearing from people about a poet and asked if they were referring to William Shakespeare or perhaps his friend Robert Lowell. "But it was James Whitcomb Riley," he said. "You could hardly expect to win under those circumstances."

Kennedy, too, had a difficult time during the early days of his campaign getting his message through to Indiana voters. Kennedy had been warned by Martin that Hoosiers were "phlegmatic, skeptical, hard to move, with a 'show me' attitude." Kennedy decided to break through voters' defensiveness by throwing himself into the campaign, barnstorming around the state in motorcades, making quiet stops at sites important to Indiana history in the southern portion of the state and even resurrecting railroad whistlestop campaigning on the Wabash Cannonball. "He always does better in person," campaign aide Fred Dutton said of the candidate. "Because Bob is so misunderstood, he has to show himself."

Kennedy's experiences with Hoosiers also influenced the candidate. John Douglas, the son of Illinois U.S. Senator Paul Douglas and a key Kennedy

Kennedy gives a short speech to a crowd at Twenty-First and Harding Streets in Indianapolis during the final days of the Indiana primary, May 4, 1968. *Indiana Historical Society.*

aide during the Indiana primary, marveled at Kennedy's ability to overcome numerous obstacles—hostile press coverage from Indianapolis newspapers, little support from local party leaders and resentment from college students opposed to the Vietnam War about his late entry into the race—through the force of his own character. "By the end of that Indiana campaign he was an attractive, effective, articulate candidate, entirely capable of presidential leadership," said Douglas.

The night before Indiana voters went to the polls, Kennedy, exhausted from a full day of campaigning that started in Evansville and ended with a nine-hour motorcade through a series of communities in northwest Indiana, stopped for an early-morning dinner at an Indianapolis restaurant with campaign aides and members of the media. Kennedy, his hands red and swollen after shaking thousands of hands, ruminated on his experiences and a decision that might end his fledgling effort at the White House once and for all. In a mellow mood, according to *Village Voice* reporter Jack Newfield, the candidate expressed a fondness for the state and its people. "I like Indiana. The people here were fair to me," Kennedy said. "I gave it everything I had here, and if I lose, then, well, I'm just out of tune with the rest of the country."

Kennedy captured the Indiana Democratic presidential primary, receiving 328,118 votes (42.3 percent) to 238,700 (30.7 percent) for Branigin and 209,695 (27 percent) for McCarthy. Winning the Indiana primary kept alive Kennedy presidential hopes. "He went yammering around Indiana," noted Martin, Indiana historian and writer, "about the poor whites of Appalachia and the starving Indians who committed suicide on the reservations and the jobless Negroes in the distant great cities, and half the Hoosiers didn't have any idea what he was talking about; but he plodded ahead stubbornly, making them listen, maybe even making some of them care, by the sheer power of his own caring." One month later, in Los Angeles, Kennedy was dead, assassinated moments after his victory in the California Democratic presidential primary.

GUS GRISSOM AND THE
FLIGHT OF *LIBERTY BELL 7*

Early in the morning on July 21, 1961, a Redstone rocket blasted off from a launch pad at Cape Canaveral in Florida. At the top of the rocket in the tiny Mercury spacecraft sat a Purdue University graduate who had earned his wings as a pilot with the U.S. Air Force, flying about one hundred combat missions during the Korean War. One of seven men selected by the federal government to become the country's first astronauts, Gus Grissom sat poised to become only the third man and second American to journey into space. His trip proved to be an eventful one.

Born and raised in Mitchell, Indiana, Grissom, the son of a railroad signalman, had turned to flying for a career after receiving a degree in mechanical engineering from Purdue. After his service in Korea, Grissom had returned to the United States and had become a test pilot at the Wright-Patterson Air Force Base near Dayton, Ohio. He was still at the Dayton facility testing aircraft like the F-104 Starfighter on October 4, 1957, when the Soviet Union shocked the world by announcing it had successfully launched the first satellite, Sputnik, into space. The 184-pound satellite, the size of a basketball, could be heard by American tracking stations as it circled the globe making its "beep-beep" sound. The space race had begun.

After a few false starts (early American rockets had the disconcerting habit of blowing up), scientists managed to put the first U.S. satellite, Explorer 1, into orbit nearly four months after the Russians' space success. As the public and politicians clamored for action, the United States initiated in 1958 its first man-in-space program, Project Mercury. President Dwight

Formal portrait of Virgil I. "Gus" Grissom, selected as one of the Original 7 Mercury astronauts. "If my country decided that I was one of the better qualified people for this new mission," Grissom said after his selection, "then I was proud and happy to help out." *National Aeronautics and Space Administration.*

Eisenhower decided that the astronauts for the space program should come from the ranks of military service test pilots, and the National Aeronautics and Space Administration asked the services to list members who met specific qualifications. Nearly 500 candidates qualified; 110 passed the initial screening process.

One of the pilots called to Washington, D.C., at the beginning of February 1959 to be evaluated as a possible astronaut was Gus Grissom, who received the top-secret news from the adjutant at Wright-Patterson, who asked him, "Gus, what kind of hell have you been raising lately?" A confused Grissom expressed puzzlement over the question and learned that he had received orders to report to Washington wearing civilian, not military, attire. Before he left home, Grissom's wife, Betty, thinking of the wildest possibility, prophetically asked him, "What are they going to do? Shoot you up in the nose cone of an Atlas [rocket]?"

Reporting to the nation's capital (he felt like he had "wandered right into the middle of a James Bond novel"), Grissom was ushered into a large reception room filled with men who were, he discovered after a brief time talking with them, fellow test pilots. From this group, a total of thirty-nine men, Grissom included, were sent to Lovelace Clinic in Albuquerque, New Mexico, to be probed and prodded by scientists. They later underwent pressure-suit tests, heat tests, acceleration tests and vibration tests at the Aeromedical Laboratory of the Wright Air Development Center in Ohio.

From this torturous process, NASA picked seven to serve as Project Mercury astronauts and presented them to the public in April 1959. The American astronauts were, from the U.S. Marine Corps, John Glenn; from the U.S. Navy, Walter Schirra, Alan Shepard and Malcolm Scott Carpenter; and from the U.S. Air Force, Donald "Deke" Slayton, Gordon Cooper and Grissom. The Hoosier flier had almost missed out on the historic designation when doctors discovered during their wide-ranging tests that Grissom suffered from hay fever. His pointed reply—"there won't be any ragweed pollen in space"—saved him from being dropped from consideration.

With his allergy problem out of the way, Grissom and his fellow astronauts underwent training to see which one, NASA confidently predicted, would be the first man in space. The astronauts, except for Glenn, seemed more at ease with training for going into space than they did with dealing with the crush of media attention on them and their families. The media scrutiny would only grow as time went by. On January 19, 1961, Robert Gilruth, head of Project Mercury, confidentially informed the astronauts of the flight order: Shepard would be the first man to ride the Redstone rocket; Grissom had the second flight; and Glenn would be the backup for both missions.

It did not work out as the American space agency had hoped; on April 12, 1961, Russian cosmonaut Yuri A. Gagarin made a one-orbit flight around the Earth that lasted 108 minutes in his Vostok spacecraft *Swallow*, winning for the Soviet Union the honor of being the first nation to put a human being into the inky void of space. Shepard followed Gagarin into space with his suborbital flight aboard *Freedom 7* on May 5, 1961.

On the morning of his scheduled flight aboard his spacecraft, designated as the *Liberty Bell 7*, Grissom appeared calm and collected. During a last-minute physical, the doctor examining Grissom was surprised at his subject's low blood pressure. Grissom's fifteen-minute, thirty-seven-second flight went off without a hitch, as his capsule made a successful splashdown in the Atlantic Ocean. From that point on, however, everything that could go wrong did go wrong.

As Grissom waited to be picked up by Marine Corps helicopters from the carrier *Randolph*, he informed the chopper pilots that he would need three or four minutes to check the switch positions on his instrument panel.

The Mercury astronauts pose in front of a U.S. Air Force F-106B aircraft. *From left to right*: Scott Carpenter, Gordon Cooper, John Glenn, Grissom, Wally Schirra, Alan Shepard and Deke Slayton. *National Aeronautics and Space Administration.*

According to the recovery plan, the helicopter pilot was supposed to radio to Grissom as soon as he had lifted the capsule from the water. At that point, Grissom would remove his helmet, blow off the hatch and exit the spacecraft. "I had unhooked the oxygen inlet hose by now and was lying flat on my back and minding my own business," Grissom recalled, "when suddenly the hatch blew off with a dull thud. All I could see was blue sky and sea water rushing in over the sill." Tossing off his helmet, the astronaut hoisted himself through the hatch. "I have never moved as fast in my life," said Grissom. "The next thing I knew I was floating high in my suit with the water up to my armpits."

Although a helicopter managed to snag the capsule, it could not handle the weight of the waterlogged spacecraft and had to cut it loose; it was the first time in his long flying career that Grissom had ever lost an aircraft. (On July 20, 1999, undersea explorer Curt Newport raised the *Liberty Bell 7* from its resting place on the ocean floor. Today, the spacecraft is

A helicopter from the USS *Randolph* attempts to lift the *Liberty Bell 7* spacecraft from the Atlantic Ocean after its hatch had malfunctioned at the end of its mission. *National Aeronautics and Space Administration.*

part of the collection of the Kansas Cosmosphere and Space Center in Hutchinson, Kansas.)

Meanwhile, the astronaut was struggling to keep from drowning. Although his spacesuit kept out the water, he was losing buoyancy because of an open air-inlet port in the belly of his suit. As he fought to stay afloat, Grissom regretted the two rolls of dimes, three one-dollar bills, two sets of pilot's wings and some miniature models of the spacecraft he had stowed in the leg pocket of his spacesuit as souvenirs of his flight. "I thought to myself, 'Well, you've gone through the whole flight, and now you're going to sink right here in front of all these people,'" Grissom recalled.

An exhausted Grissom finally managed to grab a horse-collar by a helicopter and found he had the strength once onboard to grab a Mae West life jacket and put it on for the flight back to the aircraft carrier. "I wanted to make certain that if anything happened to this helicopter I would not have to go through another dunking," he said. Once Grissom was safely onboard the *Randolph*, an officer came up to him and handed him his space helmet,

A wet Grissom walks on the deck of the carrier *Randolph* on his way to a physical checkup following his dunking in the ocean. *National Aeronautics and Space Administration.*

which had been plucked from the water by the crew of an escort destroyer. "For your information," the officer told the astronaut, "we found it floating right next to a ten-foot shark."

After his harrowing near drowning, Grissom had enough composure to call his wife from Grand Bahama Island. A relieved Betty Grissom lightheartedly informed her husband that she had heard he had "got a little bit wet."

Moving on to more serious matters, she asked him the crucial question: had he done anything wrong that contributed to the capsule's sinking? "I did not do anything wrong," Grissom emphatically replied. "That hatch just blew." With that matter resolved for the moment, the astronaut calmly ended the conversation by asking his wife to bring some extra slacks and shirts with her when she met him in Florida.

Although an accident review panel cleared Grissom and the other astronauts supported him, unanswered questions about the hatch dogged the Hoosier native for the rest of his career. In Thomas Wolfe's book *The Right Stuff* and the movie of the same name based on the work, the author and filmmaker insinuated that Grissom panicked and had been to blame for the hatch coming off ahead of schedule. According to astronaut Gordon Cooper, these allegations were false. "He [Grissom] did not screw up and lose his spacecraft," Cooper said. "Later tests showed the hatch could malfunction, just as Gus said it did. A vacuum built up in the firing pin channels."

Sam Beddingfield, a NASA engineer responsible for the pyrotechnics and recovery system on the Mercury capsule and a friend of Grissom's who believed in the astronaut's courage and poise, thoroughly investigated the incident and discovered two ways in which the hatch could have blown in the manner described by Grissom. Even the actor who plays the unlucky astronaut in the movie *The Right Stuff*, Fred Ward, expressed doubt about Grissom blowing the hatch on purpose. Ward had learned that all the astronauts who did blow their hatches suffered bruised knuckles, and Grissom's knuckles were not bruised. "I think NASA sort of pointed the finger at him to take the blame off themselves for losing the capsule," Ward said. "I don't think he was responsible at all."

NASA must have agreed, as it tapped Grissom and John Young to test out the new two-man Gemini spacecraft on its maiden voyage into space on a three-orbit mission on March 23, 1965. The agency also selected Grissom to command the first manned Apollo mission, one of the initial steps on the way to meeting President John F. Kennedy's goal of landing a man on the moon and returning him safely to Earth before the end of the decade. Deke Slayton, responsible for selecting flight crews, privately told his friend Grissom that if all went well, the Hoosier native would be first in line to command a lunar mission.

All did not go well. On Friday, January 27, 1967, Grissom and his crewmates—Roger Chaffee, a rookie and the youngest person ever selected to join the astronaut corps, and Ed White, the first American to walk in space—

The crew of the ill-fated Apollo 1 mission that lost their lives in the January 27, 1967 fire: (left to right) Ed White, Grissom and Roger Chaffee. *National Aeronautics and Space Administration.*

were involved in a simulated countdown of the three-man Apollo spacecraft at the Kennedy Space Center's Pad 34. At one o'clock in the afternoon, the astronauts and Hoosier native Gus Grissom, the first American to fly in space twice, entered the Apollo command module, built by North American Aviation. They never made it out alive. At 6:31 p.m., flight controllers on the ground heard an astronaut, probably Chaffee, calmly announce, "Fire. I smell fire." Seconds later, White more urgently stated, "Fire in the cockpit."

The intense heat and smoke hampered rescue efforts, but pad workers finally were able to open the hatch. They were too late; the three astronauts were dead, killed not by the fire but by the carbon monoxide that filled the cabin and entered their spacesuits after flames had burned through their air hoses. Doctors treated twenty-seven men involved in the rescue attempt for smoke inhalation. Two were hospitalized.

It took NASA more than a year after the accident, during which time the spacecraft underwent extensive modification, to launch another manned mission. Apollo 7, commanded by Grissom's friend Wally Schirra, an original Mercury astronaut, made 163 orbits during its eleven-day mission in the redesigned command module; America was back on its way to the moon.

Looking back on the tragedy from a perspective of many years, NASA flight director Chris Kraft noted that while it was "unforgivable that we allowed that accident to happen," if it had never occurred America would not have gone to the moon when it did. "We made a lot of changes to the command and lunar modules as a result of that experience," Kraft said. "I think we would have had all kinds of trouble getting to the moon with all the systems problems we had. That terrible experience also brought a new resolve and a renewed commitment to get the job done."

It was Grissom himself, however, who perhaps best summed up the feelings of the astronauts, many of them test pilots used to losing friends in the line of duty: "If we die, we want people to accept it, and hope it will not delay the space program. The conquest of space is worth the risk of human life."

THE HOOSIER SLIDE

At eleven o'clock on a Wednesday morning in 1930, government dignitaries and civic leaders gathered to lay the cornerstone for a structure that represented, according to an editorial writer for the *Michigan City News*, "a new industrial era" for the city: a $9 million generating plant for the Northern Indiana Public Service Company. The writer envisioned the "location of many splendid industries in Michigan City," attracted by the availability of cheap power, a good transportation system and the city's central location in the United States.

Buried in the *News*'s description of the event was the information that the station occupied a tract of land formerly home to one of the area's notable landmarks: the giant sand dune known as the Hoosier Slide. Today, nothing is left of the mountain of sand that could be seen as far away as Chicago and managed, year after year, to attract countless tourists to its slopes.

The spectacular view of Lake Michigan offered by dunes such as the Hoosier Slide provided a powerful enticement to early travelers. In 1836, Englishwoman Harriet Martineau, a writer traveling from Detroit to Chicago, stopped in Michigan City to see Lake Michigan. Although she had to endure wet weather and bad roads on her journey, when she finally made it into Michigan City what she saw impressed her, especially her splendid view of the lake. Upon arriving in the city, Martineau and a traveling companion "were anxious to see the mighty fresh water sea." The two ran up a dune covered with pea vine and beheld what they had traveled so far to see. Martineau noted, "The whole scene stands insulated in my memory, as absolutely singular; and, at this distance of time, scarcely credible. I was so well aware on the spot that it would be so, that I made careful and copious notes of what I saw; but memoranda have nothing to do with such emotions as were caused by the sight of that enormous body of tumultuous waters, rolling in apparently upon the helpless forest—everywhere else so majestic."

William Woodward, who had come to Michigan City in the 1840s to work in a general store, painted a less flattering picture of the town. Writing back to his brother in Middletown, Connecticut, Woodward complained that "M. City is the homliest [*sic*] place in the world, I suppose, or at least I never saw a worse looking one." He went on the say that the community was "built on the sand where nothing will grow and I have not seen such a thing as a garden here."

Although all Woodward could see was sand, more enterprising merchants saw the gritty substance as something else—a gold mine. By the 1890s, the Hoosier Slide, along with the Indiana State Prison, attracted tourists from Chicago, Lafayette, Peru, Indianapolis and other towns. The Monon, Lake Erie and Western and Michigan Central railroad lines lured passengers to Michigan City by touting the Hoosier Slide's beauty and its panoramic view of Lake Michigan. Even those just passing through on trains were awed by the Hoosier Slide's size. Writing about the sand hill, Carter H. Manny,

Visitors scramble to the top of the giant Hoosier Slide. Sand from the dune was used by a variety of companies, including Muncie's Ball Brothers. The sand gave the firm's jars their distinctive blue color. *Indiana Historical Society, P0411.*

whose father, William B. Manny, would be one of the first to see the potential industrial uses for Hoosier Slide, noted that "some people from afar who passed through in the winter time often inquired of the railroad men how such a big pile of snow got there."

Several excursion steamers also made Michigan City a main destination. Ships such as the *Theodore Roosevelt, United States, Indianapolis, Soo City, City of Grand Rapids* and *Christopher Columbus* brought countless visitors to Michigan City's shores. The *Michigan City News* announced on August 17, 1887, that six hundred tourists, after working up an appetite while seeing the sights, had dined at Shultz's restaurant. Gladys Bull Nicewarner, in her history of the city, reported that on one day (July 25, 1914) six steamers brought nearly ten thousand people to see the northwest Indiana community's attractions.

To entice more and more tourists to their fair city, Michigan City merchants offered merchandise and cash prizes for races up the giant sand pile's slopes and even held marriage ceremonies on its peak. An Indiana State Prison official, hoping to attract visitors from southern Indiana, offered a free marriage license, minister and excursion to any couple who would be willing to exchange their wedding vows on Hoosier Slide. A Mr. Plasterer, a southern Indiana farmer, and his bride-to-be accepted the offer, and many residents and excursionists trooped up the sandy slopes to witness the happy occasion.

A local newspaper reported that after the ceremony was completed, the minister offered a poem to the newlyweds:

> *To you, who now stand side by side,*
> *On this, the top of Hoosier Slide,*
> *I have pronounced you man and wife,*
> *As long as you both shall live this life,*
> *Now, Mr. and Mrs. Plasterer,*
> *Shun the ways which lead to disaster,*
> *And choose the path, which Christ has given,*
> *The path which leads from earth to heaven.*

In addition to marriages, the towering sand dune hosted hill-climbing contests, firework shows and wrestling and boxing matches. "There always seemed to be human beings here and there on its slopes and top during all seasons of the year," said Carter Manny. Daredevil youngsters used wooden toboggans and hand-fashioned metal sheets to slide down the hill during winter and summer. The ship captains who brought tourists and freight to Michigan City also depended on the landmark.

The beginning of the end for Hoosier Slide came in the late 1890s. From time to time, the Monon Railroad, which ran a switch track alongside Hoosier Slide's eastern slope, received requests from a downstate Monon agent for Michigan City sand. It was used to sand railroad tracks for better traction. This development caught the attention of William Manny, who worked for the line for a number of years and grew up in Michigan City. Manny and I.I. Spiro, a local lawyer, began purchasing large amounts of lakefront land, believing that the region was ripe for industrial development. Hoosier Slide was part of this property, and in 1906, Manny incorporated the Hoosier Slide Sand Company. The giant sand dune's death warrant had been signed.

Hoosier Slide's destruction was aided by the industrial boom that occurred after the discovery of extensive supplies of natural gas in central Indiana in the mid-1880s. Cities such as Muncie, Anderson, Kokomo, Richmond and others were soon besieged with new factories wanting to take advantage of this cheap natural resource. Glass companies—for example Ball Brothers in Muncie and the Pittsburgh Plate Glass Company in Kokomo—sent north for Michigan City sand to help manufacture their products.

Glass factories were not the only concerns clamoring for sand, according to Carter Manny, who upon his return from college in 1912 took over the sand business from his father. Manny, who faced competition from another firm—the Pinkston Sand Company, which was served by the Michigan Central Railroad—filled orders not only from Indiana businesses but also from companies as far away as Massachusetts and Mexico. Hoosier Slide sand was used for making glass insulators for telegraph and telephone poles, cores in iron foundries and sand beaches for lakes and municipal bathing areas; it was even used as a fill for sand traps at Hoosier humorist George Ade's private golf course in Kentland, Indiana.

In the beginning, workers known as dockwallopers loaded the sand onto freight cars using wheelbarrows, planks and shovels. Eventually, the sand was loaded through a system using tracks and small dump cars. The new system, however, did create a problem. Although the dump cars were chained down after work was over, youngsters sneaked into the area, broke locks and took joyrides down the tracks. "I recall that when I visited this spot one Sunday afternoon with my father," said Carter Manny, "we arrived just in time to see one of these cars loaded with boys come barging down the trestle and across its end to fall on the other side of the freight tracks below." Luckily, the young daredevils escaped injury, but that was not always the case for the workers. Manny remembered a particularly dry stretch of weather when sand became loose at the top and "came cascading down and caught one of the loaders, covering him with tons of sand for which he could not be dug before his life had been smothered away."

As the sand operation grew, the railroad tracks encompassed the Hoosier Slide's northeast corner and traveled down around its north side, which faced Lake Michigan. Between the tracks and the lake, a small village of sand workers sprouted. "It was a hard life, but one seemingly enjoyed by the people," Manny noted. During the winter, when frigid blasts whipped shoreward from Lake Michigan carrying cutting sand particles, the dockwallopers' enjoyment of life perhaps lessened considerably.

Manny implemented more efficient mining methods when he took over the business from his father in 1912. Within two years, the Hoosier Slide Sand Company had become the first firm to purchase a small locomotive crane to load the sand. Manny also experimented with a machine, powered by electricity, that tossed the sand back into the ends of the boxcars. The era of the dockwalloper was coming to an end.

By the early 1920s, the Hoosier Slide Sand Company, in conjunction with the Pinkston Sand Company, had managed to level what had once been Michigan City's main landmark. With the demise of the giant dune, Manny moved his sand operation west of the former Hoosier Slide to virgin duneland. The leveled land was eventually sold by the Pinkston and Hoosier Slide companies to NIPSCO as the site for its power generating station.

The amount of sand moved in the years since the first shovel broke the ground is a matter of conjecture. Some have estimated the amount at approximately 13.5 million tons (based on 50 tons of sand per railroad car and three hundred shipping days per year over a thirty-year period). Manny, however, who had years of on-site experience, believed that estimate to be "exaggerated" and placed the total tonnage at 9 million, which he based on a twenty-year period of removal.

Whatever the total amount removed, the result was the same—Hoosier Slide was gone. For today's visitors to Michigan City's lakefront, all that remains are the photographs and memories.

LOST AT SEA

NORMAN H. VANDIVIER AND THE BATTLE OF MIDWAY

T he first telegram from the U.S. Navy Department arrived at the Franklin, Indiana farm of Fred and Mary Vandivier early in the morning on June 17, 1942. On it were the words that every parent who had a family member serving in the armed forces during World War II feared—their eldest son, Norman, had been killed in action. The navy pilot had been flying a mission from the aircraft carrier USS *Enterprise* against the Japanese somewhere in the Pacific thirteen days earlier in an engagement that became known as the Battle of Midway, a smashing and needed triumph for American forces. While the grief felt by the parents of the Franklin College graduate was still fresh, they received a second dispatch informing them that the first telegram has been mistaken; their son was not dead, but instead had been listed as missing in action.

The scrambled communications from Washington, D.C., had the pilot's frantic parents searching for answers from anyone they could find who knew their son. Following up on a letter from Lieutenant L.A. Smith, the commanding officer of Bombing Squadron 6 (the group in which Norman flew), which had confirmed that Norman had been forced down at sea, Fred Vandivier wrote Smith on June 29 noting that "this uncertainty and anxiety of waiting is very distressing."

Fred wrote that his wife, who suffered with a stomach ulcer, "has so reacted to this news that she is seriously ill." Norman had not been home for a visit since Christmas 1940, so his father sought some personal information from his squadron mates in order to ease the pain felt by him and his wife. "Did he fit in?" Fred asked about his son. "Was he happy? Did he have ability? Did he have confidence in himself? Does anyone know of his last flight? Did he fly alone? If he doesn't show up within the next few days, what do you think was his most probable fate?"

The anxious Hoosier father had to wait some time for answers to his questions. What has emerged over the many years since the end of the war is a picture of a young man who had a talent for his chosen profession, especially the difficult task of flying the navy's Douglas SBD Dauntless dive bomber against the enemy's ships and shore installations. What he had little use for, however, was the navy's spit-and-polish traditions. He wrote to his sister, Rosemary, a Rushville teacher, during his training that he had become tired of what he called "this 'Yes, Sir,' business."

In the sheaf of letters he wrote to his family, now part of the Indiana Historical Society's William Henry Smith Library's collection, another aspect of his character shines through: a sincere desire to spare his parents from the real danger he faced, even while undergoing training at the U.S. Naval Air Station in Pensacola, Florida. He went as far as hiding from them the death of a classmate who went into a spin while in the air and never recovered, slamming into the ground. Much later, while serving in combat, he broke down and admitted to his mother and father, after the death in a crash of a friend from Johnson County, that he, too, preferred to be killed instantly in such a manner. "When the time comes, I really think that is the best way there is to go," he wrote on May 27, 1942, just a week before his own disappearance. "Of course, we all hate to think about it, and we all want to put it off as long as possible, but when the time comes, I'm sure that is the way I'd choose."

Born on March 10, 1916, in Edwards, Mississippi, Norman Francis Vandivier spent little time in that state, as his father left his position as superintendent of the Southern Christian Institute, a school for African American students, to move to Franklin in Johnson County, Indiana, running a farm located about six miles southwest of the city. Graduating from high school in 1934, Vandivier attended Franklin College, where he joined the Sigma Alpha Epsilon fraternity and starred as an end on the football squad and first baseman, pitcher and captain for the baseball team. During his time at the college, Vandivier also displayed an interest in the military, serving with the Indiana National Guard as a member of Battery A, 139th Field Artillery. Mary Vandivier said her son had a longtime interest in the military, as well as airplanes—an interest he followed after graduating from Franklin by enlisting with the U.S. Navy in the summer of 1939.

The five-foot, ten-inch, 174-pound Vandivier reported for elimination flight training as a seaman, second class, at the U.S. Naval Air Reserve Base at Grosse Ile, Michigan, on July 15, 1939. He received from the navy its standard allotment to aviation recruits of four pairs of underwear, three shirts, three pairs of pants, three pairs of socks, one new pair of shoes, a flight jacket, a helmet and goggles. After just a few hours of instruction, Vandivier expressed his confidence that he had the necessary aptitude and skills for flying. "I believe I could take one [plane] up and land it by myself," he boasted in a letter to his parents, "although I haven't ever done it yet. I have had all the controls on a flight or two but the instructor would join in once in awhile when he thought he was needed. I don't think I'm going to have any trouble and I sure do like flying."

A portrait of Norman H. Vandivier in his U.S. Navy dress uniform. *Indiana Historical Society, M0828.*

In addition to getting used to being in the air, Vandivier and his other classmates endured learning Morse code and the tedious task of cleaning all the airplanes after flights, using gasoline "to take off the oil and bug spots." Every third night, he had to go on watch from 6:00 p.m. to 10:00 p.m., staying in the hangar to answer the telephone that, thankfully, seldom rang. On August 4, he successfully soloed and received the ritual dunking in a nearby lake to mark the occasion. "You now have an aviator in the family. Boy! Do I feel good," Vandivier wrote.

After surviving his initial training regimen, Vandivier received orders to report to the Naval Air Station at Pensacola, Florida, for further training as an aviation cadet with the U.S. Naval Reserve. His orders came shortly after Nazi Germany's invasion of Poland on September 1, 1939, which had sparked declarations of war from the Allied powers, Great Britain and France, starting World War II. As American opinion vacillated from aiding Great Britain to remaining neutral in the conflict, Vandivier arrived at the Florida base in late October 1939 to be greeted with an unusual welcome. When Vandivier and other cadets walked up to the barracks that served as their home for the next several months, suitcases in their hands, someone opened a window on the third floor, beat on the screens with his fists and screamed, "Let me out of here! I want out of here! I'm starved!" Other faces appeared at various windows to yell at the newcomers "Sucker!," "So you want to be a birdy" and other choice expressions.

In addition to the harassment from his more experienced classmates, Vandivier had to suffer through a long day of lectures on seamanship, naval leadership, fundamentals of the naval service and naval command and procedure. His day started at 5:00 a.m. and ended at 9:00 p.m. "That's about as long as it is on the farm," he noted. "There is a lot of pressure on you all the time, too."

The pace never seemed to let up over the next few months, as Vandivier practiced his marksmanship with machine guns, learned how to fly a variety of maneuvers (snap rolls, loops, wing-overs, cartwheels and figure eights) in a Stearman-built NS1 airplane, developed a knack for formation flying, took to the skies in actual combat aircraft used by the navy and had his normal flying senses challenged by learning to fly only by instruments in a blacked-out cockpit. "Their speedy program has made it really a case of survival of the fittest," Vandivier wrote to his parents on November 19, 1939, "and fellows keep busting out [failing] every few days. I still have plenty of confidence that I'll get along all right, but I see how a few members of the class could break out and not be missed, at least by the standards that I judge by."

As Vandivier progressed further and further into his training, his schedule tightened. In May 1940, he outlined a typical day's schedule as part of the advanced training in Squadron 5. Roused out of sleep at five o'clock in the morning, Vandivier had to eat, bathe and shave before reporting to work at his squadron at 6:30 a.m. He and his classmates pushed their airplanes out of their hangars to warm up their engines. For about two hours, he flew his low-wing aircraft by instruments before returning to the station for an hour solo flying in a North American Texan T-6 advanced trainer (an SNJ in navy parlance), which Vandivier called "the best kind of airplane they have down here," with retractable landing gear, flaps and a closed cockpit. At 12:15 p.m., he spent an hour of flight simulation on the ground in a Link Flight Trainer before another hour of solo flying in the SNJ followed by an additional hour in the Link Trainer. During this time, he was also supposed to sandwich in a radio operations exam, with eight minutes of sending and eight minutes of receiving without more than five mistakes. Although his day's work ended at 4:30 p.m., Vandivier said he much preferred an "easy day down on the farm digging ditches or pitching wheat. It wouldn't be nearly the strain."

In June 1940, Vandivier received a commission as an ensign, and the navy assigned him to become a member of Bombing Squadron 6 on the USS *Enterprise*, a 19,800-ton Yorktown-class aircraft carrier originally commissioned by the navy in May 1938 and a ship that provided stellar service in Pacific battles throughout World War II. To reach his new assignment, Vandivier had to travel to San Diego, California, and from there ship out on the battleship USS *Utah* for a two-week cruise to the Hawaiian Islands, where the *Enterprise*, known lovingly by its crew as the "Big E," was then stationed. "I get a big kick out of standing on deck and just looking at the water, with the snow-white foam about the boat and the water that looks exactly like ink, it is so dark blue," said Vandivier, who also told his parents he had not suffered yet from any sea sickness on the voyage.

By August, Vandivier had joined the *Enterprise*'s more than two-thousand-member crew and had begun one of the most difficult aspects of his training as a naval aviator: learning the intricacies of landing and taking off of a ship underway at sea. At first, he practiced with a landing signal officer (the crewman who guided pilots to their landings using reflective paddles) at a small airfield. The first time he witnessed a landing on his new ship, Vandivier expressed amazement at how much a ten-thousand-pound aircraft could bounce six feet in the air before finally coming to a halt, snagged by the ship's arrester cables. "You bring the plane in on full power at a very low speed, about two miles per hour above stalling speed," he explained the proper procedure in a letter to his parents. "Then, when the signal officer gives you the cut, you cut the gun and practically fall through the deck. There are nine wires stretched across the deck at 10 [foot] intervals, each about a foot above the deck, and fastened to a hydraulic cylinder, so that they will give when your hook catches. There is a hook about four feet long in the tail of the plane which we let down to catch the wire. It usually catches before any other part of the plane touches the deck and it just stops it in mid-air."

To qualify, Vandivier had to make seven landings and takeoffs on a deck made of Douglas fir from the Pacific Northwest and measuring approximately 60 feet wide and 180 feet long. "I made a fairly good approach," Vandivier said of his first landing, "got the cut [signal from the LSO], and started to settle towards the deck without any idea of what was going to happen next. I was a little too high; and got a cross wind which drifted me across the deck straight towards the tower." While only forty feet away from the tower and traveling at seventy miles per hour, Vandivier thought he might be headed

The USS *Enterprise*'s flight deck is crowded with planes in this 1939 photo. The Yorktown-class carrier had an illustrious record in the Pacific during World War II, participating in the Battle of Midway, the Battle of the Philippine Sea and the Battle of Leyte Gulf. *Official U.S. Navy Photo, National Archives and Records Administration.*

for a crash when the tailhook on his plane caught the cable "and really jerked me to a stop. Boy, was that a relief." Just a few weeks later, Vandivier had sixty-five hours of flight time and twenty carrier landings to his credit.

As a member of Bombing Squadron 6, Vandivier also had to learn how to control his plane when dive bombing, practicing this specialized skill on a target raft towed by another ship. In an October 14, 1940 letter to his parents, he outlined the "interesting problem" of targeting a bomb on a moving object. "You have to allow for the trail of the bomb, depending on the steepness of the dive and the altitude at which you release," he said. "You also allow for the distance the raft will travel after the bomb is released and the amount and direction of the wind, with its effect on the path of the bomb. All in all, you are fairly busy as you travel down at 300 miles per hour. We start our dives at 10,000 [feet] and pull out at 1,000." He called such training "fun, and an interesting game. Of course I'm glad it's just a game instead of something more serious."

To Vandivier, that something more serious that might bring him into combat involved what was going on in the Atlantic Ocean, where the

Group portrait of the *Enterprise*'s Bombing Squadron 6. Vandivier is in the back row, third from left. *Indiana Historical Society, M0828.*

American navy had established a Neutrality Patrol in the Caribbean and two hundred miles off the coasts of North and South America to deter German U-boats from interfering with shipping. If called into action there, however, Vandivier expressed doubts about the navy's chances. "As for us, we would be out of luck trying to compete with any of the modern planes being used in Europe with the planes we have," he wrote. "The U.S. has sold all of its modern planes to England and let the Navy use planes from four to ten years old. We expect to get some modern planes pretty soon." As for the threat of a possible attack by the Japanese in the Pacific, Vandivier believed that once the United States called "the Japs bluff they will back down again. They seem to be scavengers who will take whatever they don't have to fight to get."

Throughout 1941, the *Enterprise* and its crew ferried men and material from the West Coast of the United States to the Hawaiian Islands. By that spring, Vandivier's squadron had begun training and getting the bugs out of the aircraft they would take to war—the Douglas SBD Dauntless, which could be used as a scout plane or dive bomber. The Dauntless became "the most successful and beloved by aviators of all our carrier types," according to naval historian Samuel Eliot Morison, as the plane sank more Japanese shipping than any other aircraft in World War II. The two-man SBDs (aircrews said the letters stood for "slow but deadly") were equipped with two fixed, forward-firing .50-caliber machine guns in the cowling and a twin .30-caliber machine gun operated by the rear gunner/radioman. "The new planes are really much easier to handle…and they will be a much nicer carrier plane," said Vandivier. "They will also carry a 1000 lb bomb and 310 gallons of gasoline. In fact, I could probably fly from here [San Diego] home with only one stop for gas, and could probably do it in the daylight hours of one day." The Dauntless proved to be a dependable combat aircraft, able to sustain considerable damage yet still bring its aircrew home safely to their ship.

Vandivier did have some trouble with his new plane. In a May 21, 1941 letter, he outlined an "interesting experience" he had during a landing on the *Enterprise* at sea off of Oahu. When he was only 250 feet from the ship's stern, his engine cut out while flying 75 feet above the water. "Under the circumstances," Vandivier said, "I couldn't do much to get it running again before it hit the water." Calling it "an embarrassing predicament," he had to make a crash landing in the water, wrecking his new plane (which he estimated cost the American taxpayers $30,000); it sank within three minutes. His crew member managed to make it into a life raft, but Vandivier had to inflate his Mae West life jacket and dogpaddle in the warm water while waiting to be picked up by a nearby destroyer. Despite his crash, Vandivier tried to minimize the dangers he faced. Writing from Pearl Harbor, the main navy base in the Hawaiian Islands, he noted that if war came "this is the safest place I can imagine to be. It is so well fortified and guarded that it would be almost impossible to take it, and it would be practically worthless to another power anyhow. The Atlantic side of the U.S. is the bad spot now."

Vandivier proved to be very wrong in his prediction. Early in the morning of Sunday, December 7, 1941, nine-year-old Joan Zuber, the daughter of a U.S. marine officer stationed at Pearl Harbor, started her day by opening the pages of a favorite book. She had just settled back to begin her reading when, out of the corner of her eye, she saw a "grayish-black column of smoke. Something was burning."

Zuber dropped her book and ran outside to see what was happening. Looking over the bushes in her yard toward Luke Field, the navy's airbase on Ford Island located in the center of the harbor, she could see smoke and flames rising into the sky, filling it with a large black cloud. Although her first thought was to run back inside the house to tell her mother what was happening, she instead remained outside. "Just then a strange plane with red balls on the sides of its body swooped low over my head, diving toward the masts of the [battleships] *West Virginia* and *Tennessee*," Zuber remembered. "What plane was that? What was it doing flying so low?"

The plane Zuber saw streaking toward the American ships was part of a force unleashed in two waves from six aircraft carriers from the empire of Japan. The surprise attack—undertaken without a formal declaration of war—by the enemy aircraft aimed to quickly swoop down and destroy the 130 vessels of the United States' Pacific fleet—ships that Japanese fleet admiral Isoroku Yamamoto, in charge of planning the strike, called "a dagger pointed at our [Japan's] throat." That "dagger" Yamamoto had been so worried about suffered horribly from the enemy onslaught on December 7. An armor-piercing bomb slammed into the battleship USS *Arizona*. The bomb sliced through the ship and ignited its forward ammunition magazine, setting off a huge explosion and killing 1,177 crew members. Although unprepared for the onslaught, American forces shot down 29 Japanese aircraft. They suffered, however, the loss of two battleships (the *Arizona* and *Oklahoma*) and severe damage to another six battleships, as well as having about 200 airplanes destroyed on the ground and about 3,500 servicemen either killed or wounded.

For Vandivier's family, some of the first words about their son's safety came from a Globe Wireless telegram from Honolulu, which read, "SAFE AND SOUND LETTER FOLLOWING LOVE NORMAN VANDIVIER." In a December 18 letter, Vandivier said that due to "unforeseen incidents," there had been a delay in his letter writing and warned that there might be periods in the future where it would be impossible for him to send any mail home for months at a time. He also warned them to expect "disaster rumors of all kinds floating around, almost all of which die when any attempt is made to verify them. Mothers worrying about me bothers me a lot more than any of the things that have happened or are going to happen out here." Even if he had wanted to pass along information on his experiences, he could not do so because mail had to be scrutinized by navy censors and "must contain no reference to what I am doing, where I am going, nor what I have seen. That doesn't leave me a lot to write about."

What Vandivier could not tell his family was that the *Enterprise* had been involved in the tail end of the Pearl Harbor attack. The carrier had been on its way back to its base after delivering Marine Fighter Squadron 211 and its complement of Grumman F4F Wildcats to Wake Island.

Although scheduled to arrive at Pearl Harbor on Saturday, December 6, bad weather delayed the *Enterprise*'s return until Sunday, December 7. The ship's Dauntless scout planes were soon under fire by Japanese Zero fighters. "Pearl Harbor is under attack by the Japanese. This is no shit!" Lieutenant Earl Gallaher radioed back to the *Enterprise*, which lost eleven pilots and nine aircraft, some brought down by panicked American anti-aircraft crews. "Before we're through with 'em, the Japanese language will be spoken only in hell!" vowed Vice-Admiral William "Bull" Halsey Jr., who had selected the *Enterprise* as his flagship.

The men of the *Enterprise* made good on Halsey's threat, hitting back at Japanese installations in the Marshall Islands, while the USS *Yorktown* struck enemy positions in the Gilbert Islands on February 1, 1942. The mission marked the first time many of the young American pilots had been in combat. Over a fourteen-hour period during the Marshall Islands mission, the *Enterprise* launched 158 sorties against the Japanese, sinking one ship and damaging eight others, including a submarine. In addition, a navy pilot had dropped a bomb that killed Rear Admiral Yatsushiro Sukeyoshi—the first Imperial Navy flag officer to be killed in the war.

During an attack with Bombing Squadron 6 against Kwajalein Island, Vandivier, despite heavy anti-aircraft fire, was credited with scoring a near-miss on a cargo vessel and a direct hit on a small Japanese barracks, winning an Air Medal for his efforts. Vandivier and his crewmates almost ran out of luck as their ship started to steam away from the danger zone. The *Enterprise* came under attack from five Japanese twin-engine bombers, one of which, heavily damaged, attempted a suicide dive into a deck crowded with planes, only to barely miss the ship.

The *Enterprise*'s aircrews continued to hone their combat skills with raids against Japanese bases on Wake and Marcus Islands. In April, the carrier provided air support for a secret strike against the Japanese home islands. On April 18, a force of sixteen normally land-based North American B-25 Mitchell bombers led by Lieutenant Colonel James Doolittle flew off the pitching deck of the USS *Hornet* to bomb Tokyo, Japan's capital city. Although the bombers did little damage, the raid boosted morale in the United States and shocked Japanese citizens, who started to doubt, as one of them remembered, that "we were invincible."

Vandivier could relate little about his combat experiences in his letters to his parents. In a March 14 letter, he noted that the job of the *Enterprise* involved keeping the Japanese from "running wild" in the Pacific. "At present the odds are a little in favor of the enemy," he wrote, "but the odds are continually swinging to our favor....When we finally get this new army into the field to stop them on land, the navy will complete wiping up their navy and the war will be over. Sounds easy, doesn't it." He appeared proud of the navy's early work against the enemy and wondered why his service chose to keep reports of these actions under wraps from the American public. "I guess it is really our job to make the news rather than to publish it," Vandivier admitted.

On May 27, 1942, in one of the last letters he ever sent, Vandivier wrote to his college friend and Franklin neighbor Harold E. Van Antwerp, who was stationed at Fort Benning in Georgia. Again, Vandivier could not give any details about his exploits in the air against the Japanese, but he did tell his friend that even though he had yet to fill his quota, he could claim "a few in the old game bag. It's even more fun, and much more interesting than shooting rabbits, cause these little rascals can shoot back at you." He added that he had approximately 1,250 hours in the air and had made 175 carrier landings. The Dauntless had proven to be a "very good carrier" plane, but Vandivier lamented its limited bomb load that necessitated additional sorties against the enemy. "I would much rather make only a few trips, and really drop something when I unload," he told Van Antwerp. "We have found that these Japs are nothing to be sneezed at, but they are really not very good shots. But even knowing that the guy is a poor shot, you still get nervous when the party lasts too long."

Incensed by the Doolittle raid, the Japanese sent a large fleet to capture Midway Island, an American possession located about 1,000 miles northwest of Honolulu, Hawaii. In addition to capturing Midway, Japanese admiral Isoroku Yamamoto hoped to draw out the American fleet for a decisive battle. On May 30, the American fleet responded to the threat, sending the *Yorktown* to sea to join the *Enterprise* and *Hornet*, on station about 235 miles northeast of Midway. A PBY Catalina flying boat spotted the Japanese invasion force about 700 miles from Midway on the morning of June 3.

The next morning, the Japanese carriers, including four of the six that had attacked Pearl Harbor, were discovered. At about 7:00 a.m., the *Enterprise* launched its planes, including that of Vandivier and his crewman, Seaman First Class Lee Edward John Keaney. Led by the carrier's group commander, Lieutenant Commander Wade McClusky, the attack formation began with thirty-three Dauntlesses; fifteen from Bombing Squadron 6, each loaded with a one-thousand-pound bomb, and eighteen from Scouting Squadron 6, loaded with one five-hundred-pound bomb and two one-hundred-pound bombs. A few hours later, the

American planes had yet to find the enemy carriers. Although low on fuel, McClusky made the momentous decision to turn his group northwest to hunt down the enemy, finding the Japanese at about 10:00 a.m. "I knew, and most everybody knew," said Ensign Lew Hopkins, who flew in the squadron's second division, "that we didn't have enough fuel to get back."

Vandivier, who flew in the third division, and other pilots from the *Enterprise* screamed down in dives to drop their bombs onto the Japanese carrier *Kaga*, while a smaller group targeted the flagship for the Pearl Harbor attack, the *Akagi*. The Japanese fleet's air cover of Zero fighters had just decimated an attack by American Douglas TBD Devastator torpedo bombers and were at a low altitude, unprepared to tackle the dive bombers as they hurtled downward. Watching the attack, American fighter pilot Jimmy Thach described the sight as looking "like a beautiful silver waterfall, those dive-bombers coming down." It is unknown if Vandivier managed to hit the carrier or if his bomb missed the target that day.

An American Douglas SBD Dauntless dive-bomber prepares to attack Japanese naval forces during the Battle of Midway. "Pearl Harbor has now been partially avenged," Admiral Chester Nimitz said after the battle. "Vengeance will not be complete until Japanese sea power has been reduced to impotence." *Library of Congress.*

The Dauntlesses from the *Enterprise* proved their worth, however, blasting the *Akagi* and *Kaga* with their ordnance and leaving them burning wrecks that had to be abandoned by their crews. Meanwhile, dive bombers from the USS *Yorktown* hit a third carrier, the *Soryu*, dooming it as well. "*Arizona*, I remember you!" cried Earl Gallaher, a member of Scouting Squadron 6. Later in the day, Dauntless aircraft from the *Enterprise* and *Yorktown* found and crippled a fourth Japanese carrier, the *Hiryu*. Japan had been put on the defensive, and "the Americans had avenged Pearl Harbor," noted a Japanese government official.

The victory did not come without a cost. After his attack run, Vandivier had joined up with other aircraft to try make it back to the American fleet. Low on fuel, however, and perhaps suffering from damage from the fierce Japanese anti-aircraft fire or relentless attacks by Zero fighters, Vandivier radioed that he intended to put his plane down at sea.

In an October 22 letter to Fred Vandivier from Tony F. Schneider, a fellow member of Bombing Squadron 6, the navy pilot said witnesses had seen Vandivier land his Dauntless in the ocean. "Whether he was seen to get into his life raft I do not know," wrote Schneider. "But from that time on there has been no word so far as I know. I checked every day for the first several weeks hoping for news." Schneider, who enclosed eight dollars he owed Vandivier in his letter, said the Hoosier had been his best friend and roommate on the *Enterprise*. "I was forced down at sea on that date myself," he noted, "and though I was fortunate enough to be rescued on the third day, the news I have been able to get about other friends less fortunate than I has been very sketchy and incomplete. I'm sorry I cannot relieve your mental anguish."

Although his parents held out hope, nothing was ever heard or seen of Vandivier or his gunner again. A year and a day after his disappearance, Vandivier, posthumously promoted to lieutenant junior grade and awarded the Navy Cross for his part in the Battle of Midway, was declared officially dead by Department of the Navy officials. In November 1943, the navy decided to name an escort destroyer then under construction for Vandivier (the ship's construction was delayed by the war's end and finally commissioned on October 11, 1955). His parents refused to accept the loss of their son. "Even this official status does not alter our hopes that Norman is by some chance still alive today," said Fred Vandivier. "Our only hopes are that he either is marooned on a distant island or is a prisoner of the Japanese. Improbable as either may be, they still enable Mrs. Vandivier and myself to keep going in the face of our sorrow."

No good news ever came, and Fred Vandivier died on February 20, 1958. Mary Vandivier, a Gold Star mother, soldiered on until her death, at age ninety-three, in 1987. For years, she placed flowers every Memorial Day on her son's grave marker at Franklin's Greenlawn Cemetery. She continued to cherish mementos from her son's life, including the Purple Heart and other medals he received for his service in the war, as well as the silver champagne bottle holder the navy presented her after she christened the ship named in his honor. "When we couldn't have him, this kind of took the place of him," she said of her keepsakes.

A GATHERING OF POSEY

THE WESTERN ASSOCIATION
OF WRITERS

Maurice Thompson, a former Confederate soldier who had moved to Crawfordsville, Indiana, in 1868, became friends with a former foe: Union general Lew Wallace. As well as sharing a law office with Wallace, Thompson also shared an appreciation for his friend's writing. In reviewing Wallace's book *The Fair God* in the *Indianapolis Journal*'s December 5, 1874 edition, Thompson praised the work as "the greatest book (the greatest novel, I should say) ever written by a native of the West." Thompson was not as kind, however, to those in the East who had disparaged Wallace's literary effort. "If the 'Fair God' had been written," Thompson claimed, "by someone of the few men of letters whom Eastern critics have, for reasons patent to themselves alone, chosen to praise at all times without stint, the book would have met with a success scarcely precedented."

Thompson's review struck a chord. Just a few days after the *Journal* printed the article, a fellow Wallace admirer chimed in with a letter to the editor agreeing with Thompson's judgment about the prejudice eastern critics had toward western writers. The letter writer, who signed himself "I.H.," had an answer: "There is one way in which it has long appeared to me the literary people of the West might give help and encouragement to each other and that is by some sort of union or association."

It took another twelve years, but the unknown letter writer's suggestion was finally acted on at a June 30, 1886 meeting in the auditorium of Indianapolis's Plymouth Church attended by about sixty men and women interested in the writing profession. "When these writers…did meet," the

Journal reported, "the assemblage, instead of being food for laughter, as some persons thought and even went so far as to say it would be, proved to be a very practical and business-like body." The Western Association of Writers had been born.

In its nearly twenty-year existence, the WAW—variously referred to as the "Literary Gravel Pit Association," "The Writer's Singing Bee," "a literary house party," "an effort to get up a corner in Spring poetry and fix the price of manuscript stories at so much per year" and other less than flattering terms by its critics—attracted to its colors such literary luminaries as Thompson (who was elected the group's first president), James Whitcomb Riley, Sarah Bolton, John Clark Ridpath, William Dudley Foulke, Meredith Nicholson, Paul Laurence Dunbar, Booth Tarkington, Will Cumback, Mary H. Catherwood and Benjamin Parker. The association's annual weeklong conventions at Spring Fountain Park on the shores of Eagle Lake near Warsaw, Indiana, brought together in one spot poets, novelists, short story writers, historians and others interested in *belles lettres*. "In the writer's view, the point of interest lay not so much in the actual literary standards of the organization as in the fact that all kinds of authors who were moved by the literary impulse, flocked together so insistently year after year," noted Indiana historian George S. Cottman, a longtime WAW member. "It was the gravitating to each other of kindred spirits who in their daily environments, found scant appreciation of the fugitive fancies that haunted them."

Inspired by the success enjoyed by such Indiana authors as Riley and Thompson, Hoosiers of all types following the Civil War were trying their hand at writing, especially poetry. "There was a time in Indiana when it was difficult to forecast who would next turn poet," observed Meredith Nicholson in his book *The Hoosiers*. One Indianapolis journalist declared that "there had appeared in the community a peculiar crooking of the right elbow and a furtive sliding of the hand into the left inside pocket, which was an unfailing preliminary to the reading of a poem." Various literary organizations sprang up to minister to those afflicted with the writing bug: the Indianapolis Literary Club in 1877, the Terre Haute Literary Club in 1881 and the Ouiatenon Club (Crawfordsville) in 1883. It was the WAW, however, that became, as one historian put it, "intimately connected with the spirit which produced the Golden Age of Indiana literature."

A Hoosier-dominated institution from its inception, the association's guiding spirit was Marie L. Andrews of Connersville, who first discussed the idea with J.C. Ochiltree, *Indianapolis Herald* editor, in the summer of 1885. Ochiltree offered Andrews a list of *Herald* contributors and prepared for her a prospectus for a literary organization. That winter, three regular writers for the *Herald*—Dr. J.N. Matthews, Richard Lew Dawson and Dr. H.W. Taylor—exchanged correspondence discussing the possibility of calling a "gathering of the poets of the Wabash Valley in some convenient city, or resort, for the purpose of enjoying whatever pleasure might result from a meeting so novel and unique," remembered Matthews. Working together, Andrews and Dawson produced a notice, addressed to "The Literary Profession," which was published on April 3, 1886, in the *Chicago Current*. The notice called on "all writers of verse and general literature" to band together to form a new literary association that aimed at discussing "methods of composition, and all topics pertaining to the advancement of literature in America."

The association's sponsors received more than one hundred positive responses to their call for action, and the first meeting was held in Indianapolis in late June 1886. "In the assembled audience," wrote a *Journal* reporter, "was a score or more of persons with enviable reputations as writers, and whose outpourings have graced the pages of volume and magazine, as well as the brighter, but perhaps more evanescent column of the newspaper."

At the 1886 meeting, Thompson was elected as the group's first president, Andrews as secretary and Ochiltree as treasurer. A subsequent gathering in October saw the organization adopt both a constitution and a name for itself: the American Association of Writers. Members agreed that the organization's main mission was to "promote acquaintance and friendship among the literary fraternity, and impart encouragement and enthusiasm to one another." The association also would work to protect writers against "piratical publishers" and would meet to hear literary work produced by its members.

Speaking at the fall gathering, Thompson warned those in attendance that a meeting involving "literary folk for the purpose of forming a close corporation is, in fact, a pretty good joke, and we ought to be thankful that so little has been said about the fine frenzy of our eyes and the cerulean tinge of our hose. When we come to think about it, we do occupy a doubtful ground, and we must be careful what airs we put on." Members took their president's words to heart and, in June 1887, decreased their horizons a bit by changing the organization's name to the Western Association of Writers, "an appellation," noted Cottman, "not so inept, since not a few who shared in membership came drifting in from beyond the borders of our state."

The WAW's early years were rocky at best, especially when it came to leadership. Members were dissatisfied with Thompson's performance as president, especially his failure to attend several meetings. Thompson's duties as state geologist often interfered with his commitment to the writers group. In the summer of 1888, the association removed him from office in favor of Parker, a Thompson friend and poet from New Castle. Thompson, whose *Hoosier Mosaics* (1875) collection had made him a popular literary figure in the state, was unhappy about the association's action. In a June 11, 1888 letter to Parker, marked private and personal, he congratulated his friend on his appointment and wished him success in the job. "I am glad that I am now perfectly free to sever my connections with the association, or, rather, I am content that the association has incontinently kicked me out of its back door," Thompson wrote. "If the association can justify such an insult as my removal without notice and with not even a chance to resign, I certainly can maintain myself in bidding a dignified *adieu* to the whole affair. Sincerely I feel relieved as I free myself and turn to a field where petty jealousies are not admitted."

With meeting attendance on the decline and feeling unappreciated in the capital city, the WAW looked for friendlier surroundings to hold its assemblies. The group found the perfect spot for its artistic endeavors in northern Indiana at a resort near Warsaw known as Spring Fountain Park Assembly on Eagle Lake (now Winona Lake). "Than this spot with its shady groves of forest trees, it profusion of gushing crystal waters, its limpid lake, and withal, its ample hotel and auditorium accommodations, nothing could be more inviting as an Arcadian setting where poets and birds alike might sing their melodious lays," said Cottman. Except for one sojourn to Dayton, Ohio, the WAW's annual convention was held at Spring Fountain Park (usually in June) from 1889 until its demise in the early twentieth century.

From the first, its new surroundings proved to be a boon for the WAW. Taking advantage of special rates offered by the Big Four Railroad Company, members competed for available spaces in the Eagle Lake Hotel (with room rates from $1.25 to $1.50 per day) and in nearby towns. During the morning and evening, those attending the convention listened to poems, stories and addresses by fellow members, while the afternoon, as the convention program stated, "will be given to recreation and social enjoyments," which included boating, fishing and swimming. Attendees at that first Eagle Lake meeting needed some relaxation after listening to such weighty addresses as "Is History a Science?" by Professor Ridpath; "Township Libraries," by then Indiana state librarian Jacob Piatt Dunn Jr.; "Ascent of the Matterhorn," by Indiana University president David S. Jordan; and "The Place of the Didactic in Poetry and Fiction" by Mary Cardwell.

Group photograph for a Western Association of Writers meeting, circa 1896, at Eagle Lake (today Winona Lake) near Warsaw, Indiana. Hoosier poet James Whitcomb Riley can be seen seated in the middle of the front row. *Indiana Historical Society, M0123.*

Cottman had found memories of the association's conventions, recalling "long sunny June afternoons when earth and sky and sparkling waters were at their best, and our genial fraternity surrendered itself to sweet-do-nothing." Usually, the WAW had the hotel mainly to itself, and its members could explore the "nooks and byways of the shady grounds" to their hearts' content, Cottman remembered. On their rambles, members could swap yarns with such noted raconteurs as Ridpath, Cumback, Fishback and Eugene Ware.

Those who preferred later hours could join a sub-organization of the WAW called Ye Owl Club, which had its first "flocking" in 1895. Led by the "Most Grand Hoo! Hoo!," the club's function was to "recuperate its members after the severe celebrations of the day. Its sessions shall be mildly orgyanic [*sic*] and of a character to cheer but not inebriate. Sessions shall not begin before 10 p.m. nor continue after cock-crow." Members of this unique group, which set dues at one cent a year, had to be ready, whenever the Most Grand Hoo! Hoo! commanded, to contribute "an impromptu song, story, recitation, hoot or other recuperative diversion." According to Cottman, Ye Owl Club ceased to be a going concern because the hotel manager refused to "allow a rebate for unused sleep."

The association's most successful conventions were those that featured its most celebrated member: Riley. "When word got around he [Riley] would be up for the annual jam session," said James Weygand in his history of the association, "its success was almost assured. Everyone knew he'd be on the program for a poem or two, and that he could be coaxed into a couple more."

Although he stood head and shoulders above most members as far as fame and talent were concerned, Riley always displayed a fond feeling for the WAW. Clara Laughlin, a Riley friend, considered most of the association convention attendees as "rather pathetic," but that view was not shared by Riley. Laughlin noted that Riley valued the would-be writers "not for what they were about to confer on a waiting world, but for what he knew it meant to those various persons *to sing* or to create unrestricted worlds of fancy and desire." The poet's muse was also stimulated by the lively gatherings in Warsaw. At one convention, Riley, inspired by the charms of a local barber's daughter, penned the following short ode: "It is the barber's daughter / And she has grown so dear, so dear / I worship e'en the lather / Her pa leaves in my ear."

Riley could sometimes be cajoled into reciting verse before the assembled association members, but his main contribution to the gathering came when the official business for the day ended. Off the hotel's main dining room, there was a room where Riley and a small group of friends often gathered to "banquet splendidly on crackers and cheese, pickles, sweet chocolate, and cold tea," Laughlin recalled. Others who shared in the camaraderie included Frank L. Stanton, an *Atlanta Constitution* staffer; Hector Fuller, *Indianapolis News* drama and literary critic; John Curtis, Bobbs-Merrill Company secretary; and Robert Burdette, a fellow poet and humorist. "Mr. Riley was always the dominating spirit," said Laughlin, "his mood the key in which our pleasure was pitched. His sensibility to the moods of others was, at times like those, extraordinary; he seemed to know infallibly when everybody was in time and tune, and when some one was ever so little off key."

As well as possessing a keen sense of appreciation for struggling authors who attended the WAW's annual conventions, Riley, who had grown rich through his work, also displayed great generosity to those not as well fixed financially. Reminiscing about the poet for the *Indiana Magazine of History*, Cottman remembered one occasion when he happened to meet Riley in Indianapolis's Bowen-Merrill bookstore shortly before the annual WAW convention. Cottman casually mentioned to Riley that Parker, a former association president "whose talent for worldly success was nil," could not attend the meeting due to a lack of funds. At once, Riley hit on a plan to bring Parker to Warsaw.

As an official of the organization, Cottman should invite the New Castle man to the convention as the association's guest and Riley would cover the railroad fare and hotel bill for the entire week. "The scheme went through," said Cottman, "but came near being amusingly embarrassing, as the recipient of the courtesy was grateful, the association knew nothing about it, and I was enjoined from telling anybody." Later, Cottman finally informed Parker about the anonymous benefactor who had provided the funds for his trip.

Riley's patronage helped keep interest high at the association's early conventions, but with his increasing popularity keeping Riley away, attendance dropped considerably as the organization moved into the new century. The aging of the WAW's founders and low annual dues (two dollars per year) were also factors that helped to speed the association's downfall. In 1904, an attempt was made to revive the moribund organization by Opie Reed, a leading figure in the Chicago Press Club. On December 16, 1904, the club sponsored a reception honoring "that great organization of writers which has taken so prominent a place in the literature of the west." Although the Chicago group brought new blood into the WAW, it could not breathe new life into the once flourishing organization.

A final attempt at resurrection was made in 1907 when a reunion of longtime members came about as the result of correspondence between Cottman and E.B. Heiney, a Huntington writer. In a February 27, 1907 letter to Cottman, Heiney lamented the WAW's death, adding that he believed the organization could be saved if enough interested members could be brought together in a central location. Cottman agreed with Heiney's plan but wrote to his friend that some revisions had to be made in the organization, especially its name. He advocated changing the WAW into the Indiana Literary Association, which, Cottman noted, "would be more modest and more conformable to its real functions. Unfortunately our old ranks are sadly broken, but cant you get some of the remnants together here and hold a conference about the matter? It really is easier to mobilize at Indianapolis than anywhere else."

On May 4, 1907, at the Claypool Hotel's Palm Room in Indianapolis, about twenty-five "literary people of Indiana," as the *Indianapolis Star* described them, met to consider the possibility of hosting a WAW conference that summer and appointed a committee to investigate. "There's been too many people getting into this association who were merely 'tuft busters' and not writers," G. Henri Bogard of Brookville told a *Star* reporter. This last-ditch effort at saving the association failed, however, and the WAW faded into obscurity.

Discerning the association's effect on the state's literary history is a difficult task. In its two decades of existence, it did produce a few volumes containing the work presented at the group's annual convention. Also, as Weygand pointed out, most of the WAW's members were "pretty small fish, but some of them grew into whales." But its greatest contribution came through its ability to provide a needed spark to the creative process for hundreds of writers in Indiana and the Midwest. There was, as Cottman noted, "nothing else in existence quite like it."

BIBLIOGRAPHY

Articles by Ray E. Boomhower (by date)

"Celebrating Statehood: Indiana's 1916 Centennial." *Traces of Indiana and Midwestern History* 3 (Summer 1991): 28–39.

"The Father of Indiana History and the Devil's Lake Monster." *Traces of Indiana and Midwestern History* 4 (Winter 1992): 38–45.

"Major General Lew Wallace: Savior of Washington, D.C." *Traces of Indiana and Midwestern History* 5 (Winter 1993): 4–15.

"The Hoosier Slide: 'Monument of Never Ending Sand.'" *Traces of Indiana and Midwestern History* 5 (Spring 1993): 12–17.

"'Nobody Wanted Us': Black Aviators at Freeman Field." *Traces of Indiana and Midwestern History* 5 (Summer 1993): 38–45.

"The Aviatrix and the University: Amelia Earhart at Purdue." *Traces of Indiana and Midwestern History* 6 (Summer 1994): 36–41.

"'To Secure Honest Elections': Jacob Piatt Dunn, Jr. and the Reform of Indiana's Ballot." *Indiana Magazine of History* 90 (December 1994): 311–45.

"Lafayette's Triumphal Return." *Outdoor Indiana* 60 (May/June 1995): 32–35.

"The Lost Astronaut: Virgil I. 'Gus' Grissom of Mitchell, Indiana." *Traces of Indiana and Midwestern History* 8 (Spring 1996): 4–15.

"Covering the Bases," *Michigan History* 80 (May/June 1996): 20–27.

"Indiana Bookshelf: The Western Association of Writers." *Traces of Indiana and Midwestern History* 15 (Spring 2003): 41–47.

"The Voters Speak: Robert F. Kennedy and the 1968 Indiana Primary." *Traces of Indiana and Midwestern History* 20 (Spring 2008): 20–29.

"The People's Choice: Indiana Congressman Jim Jontz." *Traces of Indiana and Midwestern History* 22 (Fall 2010): 14–29.

"A Slow Death: Norman F. Vandivier and the Battle of Midway." *Traces of Indiana and Midwestern History* 24 (Fall 2012): 14–25.

Books by Ray E. Boomhower (by date)

Jacob Piatt Dunn, Jr.: A Life in History and Politics. Indianapolis: Indiana Historical Society, 1997.

Destination Indiana: Travels through Hoosier History. Indianapolis: Indiana Historical Society, 2000.

"But I Do Clamor": May Wright Sewall, A Life, 1844–1920. Indianapolis: Guild Press of Indiana, 2001.

Gus Grissom: The Lost Astronaut. Indianapolis: Indiana Historical Society Press, 2004.

The Sword and the Pen: The Life of Lew Wallace. Indianapolis: Indiana Historical Society Press, 2005.

Fighting for Equality: A Life of May Wright Sewall. Indianapolis: Indiana Historical Society Press, 2007.

Robert F. Kennedy and the 1968 Indiana Primary. Bloomington: Indiana University Press, 2008.

Fighter Pilot: The World War II Career of Alex Vraciu. Indianapolis: Indiana Historical Society Press, 2010.

The People's Choice: Congressman Jim Jontz of Indiana. Indianapolis: Indiana Historical Society Press, 2012.

Dispatches from the Pacific: The World War II Reporting of Robert L. Sherrod. Bloomington: Indiana University Press, 2017.

Mr. President: A Life of Benjamin Harrison. Indianapolis: Indiana Historical Society Press, 2018.

Articles

Bourdon, Jeffrey Normand. "Trains, Canes, and Replica Log Cabins: Benjamin Harrison's 1888 Front-Porch Campaign for the Presidency." *Indiana Magazine of History* 110 (September 2014): 246–69.

Cottman, George. "John Brown Dillon: The Father of Indiana History." *Indiana Magazine of History* 1 (1905): 3–8.

———. "The Western Association of Writers: A Literary Reminiscence." *Indiana Magazine of History* 29 (September 1933): 187–97.

Dozer, Donald Marquand. "Benjamin Harrison and the Presidential Campaign of 1892." *American Historical Review* 54 (October 1948): 49–77.

Hill, Herbert R. "Memorial to a Hoosier Astronaut." *Outdoor Indiana* 46 (September 1981): 23–29.

Hoy, Suellen. "Governor Samuel M. Ralston and Indiana's Centennial Celebration." *Indiana Magazine of History* 71 (September 1975): 245–66.

Pierson, William D. "The Origin of the Word 'Hoosier': A New Interpretation." *Indiana Magazine of History* 91 (June 1995): 189–96.

Webb, Stephen H. "Introducing Black Harry Hoosier: The History Behind Indiana's Namesake." *Indiana Magazine of History* 98 (March 2002): 30–41.

Books

Boller, Paul F., Jr. *Presidential Campaigns*. New York: Oxford University Press, 1984.

Burrin, Frank K. *Edward Charles Elliott, Educator*. West Lafayette, IN: Purdue Research Foundation, 1970.

Calhoun, Charles W. *Benjamin Harrison*. New York: Times, 2005.

———. *From Bloody Shirt to Full Dinner Pail: The Transformation of Politics and Governance in the Gilded Age*. New York: Hill and Wang, 2010.

———. *Minority Victory: Gilded Age Politics and the Front Porch Campaign of 1888*. Lawrence: University Press of Kansas, 2008.

Catchpole, John. *Project Mercury: NASA's First Manned Space Programme*. Chichester, UK: Springer-Praxis Books, 2001.

Davis, Benjamin O., Jr. *Benjamin O. Davis, Jr., American: An Autobiography*. Washington, D.C.: Smithsonian Institution Press, 1991.

DiNicola, M. Travis, and Zachary Roth, eds. *Indy Writes Books: A Book Lover's Anthology*. Indianapolis, IN: Indy Reads Books, 2014.

Dooley, Brian. *Robert F. Kennedy: The Final Years*. New York: St. Martin's Press, 1996.

Dunn, Jacob P., Jr. *The Word Hoosier*. Indianapolis, IN: Bobbs-Merrill Company, 1907.

Earhart, Amelia. *Last Flight*. New York: Harcourt, Brace and Company, 1937.

Elder, Donald. *Ring Lardner: A Biography*. Garden City, NY: Doubleday, 1956.

Fisher, Jerry M. *The Pacesetter: The Untold Story of Carl G. Fisher*. Fort Bragg, CA: Lost Coast Press, 1998.

Fuller, A. James. *Oliver P. Morton and the Politics of the Civil War and Reconstruction*. Kent, OH: Kent State University Press, 2017.

Gould, Lewis L. *1968: The Election that Changed America*. Chicago: Ivan R. Dee, 1993.

Gray, Ralph D. *Indiana's Favorite Sons, 1840–1940*. Indianapolis: Indiana Historical Society, 1988.

Grissom, Betty, and Henry Still. *Starfall*. New York: Thomas Y. Crowell Company, 1974.

Gugin, Linda C., and James E. St. Clair, eds. *The Governors of Indiana*. Indianapolis: Indiana Historical Society, in cooperation with the Indiana Historical Bureau, 2006.

Hearn, Chester G. *Carriers in Combat: The Air War at Sea*. Mechanicsburg, PA: Stackpole Books, 2005.

Lardner, Ring. *The Story of a Wonder Man: Being the Autobiography of Ring Lardner*. Westport, CT: Greenwood Press, 1975.

Lindley, Harlow, ed. *The Indiana Centennial, 1916*. Indianapolis: Indiana Historical Collections, 1919.

Lovell, Mary S. *The Sound of Wings: The Life of Amelia Earhart*. New York: St. Martin's Press, 1989.

Madison, James H. *Hoosiers: A New History of Indiana*. Bloomington: Indiana University Press; Indianapolis: Indiana Historical Society, 2014.

———. *Indiana through Tradition and Change: A History of the Hoosier State and Its People, 1920–1945*. Indianapolis: Indiana Historical Bureau and Indiana Historical Society, 1982.

Martin, John Bartlow. *Indiana: An Interpretation*. Reprint, Bloomington: Indiana University Press, 2016. Originally published in 1947.

McKee, Irving. *"Ben-Hur" Wallace: The Life of General Lew Wallace*. Berkeley: University of California Press, 1947.

McPherson, James M. *Battle Cry of Freedom: The Civil War Era*. New York: Oxford University Press, 1988.

Morsberger, Robert E., and Katharine M. Morsberger. *Lew Wallace: Militant Romantic*. New York: McGraw-Hill, 1980.

Munger, Elizabeth. *Michigan City's First Hundred Years*. Reprint, [Michigan City, IN:] Michigan City Historical Society, 1990. Originally published in 1969.

Newport, Curt. *Lost Spacecraft: The Search for Liberty Bell 7.* Ontario, Canada: Apogee Books, 2002.

Osterman, Louis. *Freeman Field and Seymour: The Home Front in Indiana.* Pamphlet, 1986.

Phillips, Clifton J. *Indiana in Transition: The Emergence of an Industrial Commonwealth, 1880–1920.* Indianapolis: Indiana Historical Bureau and Indiana Historical Society, 1968.

Putnam, George P. *Soaring Wings: A Biography of Amelia Earhart.* New York: Harcourt, Brace and Company, 1939.

Riker, Dorothy, ed. *The Hoosier Training Ground.* Bloomington: Indiana War History Commission, 1952.

Shepard, Alan, and Deke Slayton. *Moon Shot: The Inside Story of America's Race to the Moon.* Atlanta, GA: Turner Publishing, 1994.

Socolofsky, Homer E., and Allan B. Spetter. *The Presidency of Benjamin Harrison.* Lawrence: University Press of Kansas, 1987.

Spector, Ronald. *Eagle Against the Sun: The American War with Japan.* New York: Free Press, 1985.

Stephens, Gail. *Shadow of Shiloh: Major General Lew Wallace in the Civil War.* Indianapolis: Indiana Historical Society Press, 2010.

Symonds, Craig L. *The Battle of Midway.* New York: Oxford University Press, 2011.

Thornbrough, Emma Lou. *Indiana in the Civil War Era, 1850–1880.* Indianapolis: Indiana Historical Bureau and Indiana Historical Society, 1965.

Vandivier, Frank E. *Jubal's Raid: General Early's Famous Attack on Washington in 1864.* New York: McGraw-Hill, 1960.

Witcover, Jules. *85 Days: The Last Campaign of Robert Kennedy.* New York: Putnam, 1969.

Wolfe, Tom. *The Right Stuff.* New York: Farrar Straus Giroux, 1979.

Yardley, Jonathan. *Ring: A Biography of Ring Lardner.* New York: Random House, 1977.

ABOUT THE AUTHOR

A native Hoosier and former newspaper reporter, Ray E. Boomhower has worked at the Indiana Historical Society since 1987, serving as editor of the society's quarterly popular history magazine, *Traces of Indiana and Midwestern History*, since 1999. He is the author of numerous articles and books on the nineteenth state, including biographies of such notable Hoosiers as Benjamin Harrison, Gus Grissom, Ernie Pyle, Lew Wallace, May Wright Sewall, John Bartlow Martin, Jim Jontz, Benjamin Harrison and Alex Vraciu. In 1998, he received the Hoosier Historian Award from the IHS, and in 2010, he was named winner of the Regional Author Award in the Eugene and Marilyn Glick Indiana Authors Awards.